MW00851079

The Last General Standing

The Last General Standing

J. Figuero

Published by: LWL Enterprises, Inc.

Inside Cover art by: Gregory Martinez

Edited by: D. Razor Babb

ISBN: 1-945484-01-2
ISBN-13: 978-1-945484-01-8

Note from the Author

I have been incarcerated for forty plus years because of the bad choices I made. Choices that have hurt a lot of people. The path I chose to follow I once believed to be an honorable, and in many ways, necessary course. As time progressed I found, however, that the gangster lifestyle was a false promise – one that inevitably leads to nothing but pain, heartbreak, and destruction.

The writing of this book is an effort to provide caution to those facing similar choices and to offer fair warning. Everything you do in life has consequences, not just for yourself, but also your kids, wife, loved ones, and the families of those you victimize along the way. To this very day because of my own actions, many are still in mourning.

I have more regrets than I can make up for in a single lifetime. Most of all, I'm filled with remorse for my actions leading to the tragic events that led to the death of my victim. The suffering I caused to his family is incalculable and forever and can't be erased. This book is a living tribute and remembrance to them all, and if it can prevent even a single occurrence of similar violence, then maybe his death won't be for nothing.

I cannot and will not tell you not to join a gang, but what this book will tell you is what will happen if you do. After reading, I hope you walk away with true insight into what it really is to live a gangster lifestyle, and understand the heavy price you'll pay.

Song of the Nuestra Familia

The Song of Nuestra Familia was produced by an unknown woman from Gilroy, who was a sympathizer and felt very compassionate toward the Nuestra Familia. She wanted to make a song about us as a family. A deal was made and she would receive 40% of the profits and the organization would receive the other 60% for their own coffers. The song was very popular and was played mostly at Mexican bars up and down the state. It sold about 100,000 copies, that is until the FBI and the SSU came down on everyone and anyone selling or playing the song. As usual, we were breaking still another law by not obtaining the proper permits and documents to make and sell the song. And because this project was gang affiliated and the fact that we were profiting from this illegally. The following are the words to this song:

Here I bring a Message
To All the Mexican People
So allow Me to Present You
My Beloved Brotherhood
Some have United
In everything and are "Familianos"

I have an Organization
Called the "Nuestra Familia"
And what a Reputation
That causes Hatred, Spite and Envy

Because of Betrayal
By some in the Family

They don't have anyone to Blame
Those that are not "Familianos"
When once they had taken an Oath
Though Their Word was lacking
That Word of Honor
That has much been Stained.

And when We Defend Ourselves,
We're accused of being Wicked
There is need of Understanding
To Defend Ourselves my Brothers
Some Fear Supporting Us
Because We are 'Familianos'

Because We are 'Familianos'
Many of Us have been Refused
Even after all We've Fought for
We're accused of being Wicked

Because the same Brothers
Have always Defrauded Us

Give me your Word my Brother
And Betray Me No More
If you need My Help
Here I am Waiting
Waiting Day after Day
For Your Hand I'll be Waiting.

There's no reason to Separate
Understand this well My Brother
Because We are Mexican People
And have Promised to be Faithful
But We will never Deny
That We are also 'Chicanos'.

Long Live the Mexican People
Not to mention all 'Chicanos'
With much Pride and Loyalty
Let My Blood run on
This says the "Nuestra Familia"
I'm not at Liberty to Lose.

Note to Readers

I want the readers to understand that I am not in any way, shape or form glorifying the gang lifestyle or the violence that takes place as portrayed in this story, nor am I condoning my part or actions as a gang member. To those of you who are considering this lifestyle, I hope you'll take this as a cautionary tale and consider how your family and loved ones will be affected. The actions and events recorded here occurred in an era when, within the prison system, a kill-or-be-killed mentality reigned ... fertile spawning grounds for the gang attitude and lifestyle. It took root, blossomed and expanded beyond what anyone could have foreseen.

Editor's Note

The study of cultural psychology suggests that whenever groups of people come together in a sustained effort towards some mutually beneficial goal or goals, they are more times than not, doing so to satisfy an innate, unstoppable, even unconscious need beyond the simplistic predilection of one's selfish struggle for resources, pleasure or prestige, and are motivated and shaped by a 'group selection' to be hive creatures who long to lose 'self' in something larger.

The "greater than 'I'" sensation is experienced (and sought out) because individuals crave and need to merge with something vast, something larger than self. In doing so it sets up a resonance pattern in the brain creating a mystical sensation or state of mind.

Humans are social creatures who need love and attachments. We are industrious with needs to enter into vital engagements toward some (subjectively) worthwhile activity and/or goal. Many times, the 'group' we are drawn into may be driven toward some pursuit of a vision of virtue, justice, or sacredness. (Of course, one group's noble purpose is sometimes another group's pure evil).

Essentially, people require love, work and a connection to something to find meaning and purpose in life, e.g., religious groups, sports, dance or exercise classes, musical orchestras, stadium events, political organizations or rallies, or military service.

A passage from the book, The Warriors: Reflections of Men in Battle, describes the thrilling communal state that soldiers sometimes enter: "I" passes insensibly into a "we", "my" becomes "our," and individual fate loses its central importance …. I believe that it is nothing less than the assurance of immortality that makes self-sacrifice at these moments so relatively easy. I may fall, but I do not die, for that which is real in me goes forward and lives on in comrades for whom I gave up my life.

Therefore, we look for something larger than self to provide a sense of purpose that is worth living, and dying for: The group. The gang.

- D. Razor Babb

Chapter 1

As I sat in the jail holding cell on that warm summer day in 1983, looking at the graffiti scratched into the walls by other souls there before me, the reality of what was happening to me set in. I'd just been sentenced to seven-years-to-life for three counts of murder and one count of conspiracy, for ordering the slaying of three rival gang members (Hits that, in reality, I knew nothing about and had no direct correlation with.) My emotions were mixed. Was I cursed? No. Did the immature choices I made have something to do with my being here? Pretty good chance. Why didn't I listen to my parents? Because I knew everything … or thought I did. I could go on with the 'What if?' scenario forever, but the bottom line was – I screwed up.

I started drifting back in time, pondering my past behavior and life that had led up to this point. My name is Joey, and this is my story ….

The first time I spent real time in prison was for auto theft, that was 1970. I was with friends at a party that was like no other. I went in with girls and beer and by the early morning hours we were all pretty inebriated. I needed a ride across town and didn't have any wheels. So, not having my senses about myself, I ventured out to find a car to take me where I needed to go. At least, that was the plan.

I wasn't familiar with the neighborhood, but happened upon a trustworthy neighbor who felt safe enough to leave the keys in his car. My evening at the party was great, and now to top it off, I was on a roll with a set of wheels to get me home. But my luck wouldn't hold. Unfortunately, my poor driving skills were observed by a traffic officer who lit up the inside of the car with red lights and a bright spot. When he walked up to the driver's side window and asked to see my license, the overwhelming smell of alcohol was a clue that a Breathalyzer wouldn't be needed. Oh, did I mention 'Rule Number One'? Never take a car from a neighborhood you're unfamiliar with and from people you don't know, even if the keys are in it.

It turned out the car I had stolen was the Chief of Police's personal car! Whoops. That explains why he was brave enough to leave the keys. The car was impounded, as was I. After reviewing my record of run-ins with the law, and other bad behavior, and before sentencing, the judge informed my lawyer he was considering sentencing me to prison for a term of six-months to five-years. The actual sentence would depend on what I did to improve myself.

I thought my attorney was joking when he told me what the judge had said. Without thinking about the consequences, I told my attorney that I'd take my chances. What did a kid like me know? I found out the hard way. I was sentenced to six-months to five-years. I had the feeling it because it was the Chief of Police's car, his personal car, that was a contributing factor and sticking point to the sentence I received.

I had no idea what lay ahead, but was soon to find out.

Chapter 2
Vacaville Reception Center

A few days after sentencing I was driven to the Vacaville Reception Center. This was the first stop. For the next thirty-to-ninety days I'd be tested and evaluated before being sent to a permanent institution to do my time.

I stepped out of the car and into a chilling fall breeze. There were dark rain clouds gathering and the air was filled with static electricity. It seemed to match both my inner uneasiness and the uncertainty of what lay before me. I was escorted to Reception and Release (R&R), where I was unshackled and had to strip down for a body search for drugs, weapons, or other contraband. I had to donate my clothing because I didn't have money to send it home. Then it was a shower, lice-spray, mandatory haircut, fingerprints, photograph, and state ID.

I was surprised and relieved to find that my cellie was someone I recognized from short stays in the California Youth Authority (CYA). 'Crackers' was also on orientation; we quickly caught up with each other on what had been going on and thirty days passed without incident. At the end of orientation, we were both cleared for GP (General Population) and moved to V-wing. We'd remain there until bused to another institution to serve out our time. We each had our own room, lots of locked doors.

When I finally hit the yard, I met a couple of older guys who had been there for a while. As it turned out, one of the guys, 'Shotgun', was a friend of my uncle. He was a drug addict and had tattoos to cover his needle marks. His partner's name was 'Babo'. Babo, a Santa Barbara born Puerto Rican, was a little buff from weight-lifting. Both of these guys had extended records and were back to prison on parole violations.

I was the youngster on the yard and new to the 'Big House'. Shotgun and Babo showed me the way around the system and the ways and rules of prison politics – what to do and not do.

It was a totally new world to me, a foreign society that I was completely unfamiliar with. I had the attitude that I just didn't care what happened. When I'd been in CYA it hadn't seemed that bad. There were rules, sure, but nothing compared to prison. Being told what to do, when to do it, how to do it didn't sit well with me. It just fueled my anger. Shotgun and Babo were a big help in keeping me steered away from particular people, certain groups and gangs. They taught me a lot of things. One of which was – no gambling. CYA was one thing, but in the penitentiary, there are older, more experienced men that have plenty of ways of getting things out of you or manipulating you into doing things you wouldn't normally do.

The ninety days were up for Shotgun and Babo. They were both sent to San Quentin Prison near San Francisco. I hated to see them go, they were both very encouraging and the wisdom they shared was invaluable. They wished me luck and we parted ways.

Over a dinner of spaghetti, salad, green peas and pudding, Crackers told me he'd seen his counselor and had been approved for Soledad Prison, North. We talked it over and knew that because of our ages we'd only be approved for one of two places – Soledad North Yard, or Deuel Vocational Institute (DVI) at Tracy. We agreed that I would try for Soledad, so at least we'd know somebody when we got there. Neither of us had been to Soledad before and knew nothing about it, except the rumors we heard around the yard. A couple of days later I was called to the counselor's office and given the choice of one of the two prisons mentioned. Two weeks later at three in the morning, twenty of us were awakened for the bus ride to Soledad Prison.

Chapter 3
Soledad Prison, North
1970

Winter was peaking and it was freezing cold. The sky was dark gray and the wind was howling, rain pelted the ground and the two-piece green jumpsuits we all wore did nothing to protect us from the weather. Steel shackles and leg irons weren't any comfort either. It was warmer on the bus though. Crackers and I sat together for the five-hour trip. After three months of being in the same place it was good to be on the road and take in some fresh scenery. At eleven o'clock we arrived at Soledad R&R. The C.O. called out our names and checked ID's, then we get a hot meal before being processed, which was a relief to our empty bellies.

R&R is a part of Soledad Central where older inmates are housed. Central has the dispensary, dental clinic, chow halls and main yard and is the main hub of the prison. The North yards are divided into four halls, or housing units, each named after a mountain. There's Rainier and Lassen on one North Yard and Shasta and Whitney Halls on the other. Each hall houses one-hundred fifty prisoners.

We were in the holding cage for four hours while they logged us into the institutional body count, then gave us two keys to our cells. One key was to lock the door from the outside when leaving. The other key was to lock the door from the inside, because in the morning all the doors are popped open for chow release, and if you didn't want to get up or go to chow, you could lock your door to prevent it from opening. It was a nice convenience, especially if you wanted to sleep in. Anyway, after the formalities were finished, seven of us were escorted to the North Yards.

Walking into Rainier Hall and looking up those three stories of cells, or, three tiers, I was reminded of a zoo. It was really noisy. The first tier was for new arrivals (fish), who have no privileges until after orientation is complete. The first tier is to be locked up (with you in your cell) at seven o'clock at night. The second tier was locked up at eight o'clock and the yard closed at nine. The third tier was locked up at ten.

For entertainment, there were two TV's mounted on the wall in the hall between adjacent (facing) tiers. It was a sort-of dayroom with benches at one end, tables and showers at the other. There were earphone jacks attached to the undersides of the benches in order to hear the TV. The speakers were disconnected because of the noise. Watching TV helped take your mind off of other things, like thinking or stressing on personal thoughts and allowed you to hold onto your sanity.

Each room (cell) was enclosed (not bars) and had windows that could be opened and closed (which are barred). I could see the green garden tool shed from my window, as well as the yard. Garden workers had access to the tool shed, which contained lawn mowers, hoses, rakes, shovels, and other garden equipment.

One morning I heard a commotion coming from the tool shed area. When I looked out my window I saw two black guys running away from the shed, and noticed a pool of blood flowing from the door that was slammed wide open in their haste to flee. Not that there was anywhere to go. A yard officer heard the racket and saw them running from the scene. He soon realized what they were running from. His complexion blanched three shades lighter when he arrived at the shed. He started blowing his whistle to summon help and alert the other officers.

We later found out that an officer had been lured to the shed on false pretenses and stabbed multiple times, his throat slashed from ear-to-ear. The facility was locked down for a few days while the murder investigation was conducted.

The adage that criminals are dumb proved to be very true in this case. Officers discovered two blood-soaked shirts in the trashcan on the second tier and the ID cards of the two inmates involved inside the shirt pockets – case closed. Both inmates were eventually found guilty of murder. They were nicknamed the Soledad Brothers from that point on. Because of the killing the tool shed was removed from the yard. I realized then that I was no longer in CYA. This was real prison where threats and action were a reality and it put the fear of God in me.

A few months went by. There were areas where we lifted weights and played marbles, basketball, cards, and chess for recreation and entertainment. Sometimes outside groups were allowed on the prison grounds. They included big-name bands like James Brown, Santana, and the Tower of Power, just to name a few. We even had a group of Christian Motorcyclists (Bill Glass) come and bring their chromed and colorful motorcycles onto the yard so we could look at them. They also brought music and offered counseling and spiritual guidance to those who asked, and for people having problems dealing with their guilty conscience and emotional pain. Having entertainment like this also helped take the anxiety away for a while and reinforced positive attitudes. A prison environment doesn't have to be negative all the time. Film projector movies were also shown in the gym. With a ten-cent movie ducat from the canteen you were allowed in for the movies. Refreshments were available, all proceeds donated to a charitable organization.

Because of the way I was sentenced (six-months to five-years), I was to be seen by the Board of Prison Terms (BPT) at a review hearing after six months. Prior to the hearing, I was given a head's up from the other inmates who had attended them on how you are treated and what to expect.

I was anxious as I entered the hearing room. There were three people (appointed by the governor) seated on one side of the table, and a single chair on the other side facing them. Before anything was said I automatically received one year more added to my time just for committing the crime. To me that was biased and just added salt to the wound. But the worst part was to come. During the hearing I let them get me angry and I lashed out and let my feelings be known. As a result, I got a second year added to my time. If, on the other hand, I'd just kept my mouth shut and not allowed the BPT people to get me pissed off, I would have just gotten a year added to my time. It's a Catch-22 situation where they win, I lose.

During the hearing, I was reminded of what I'd done and how low-down and despicable I was as a person, and basically made to feel like the lowest person on earth. I was thoroughly degraded and disheartened and told I was not fit for parole.

When they were done with me I felt as though I was a serial killer instead of a car thief. Maybe the Police Chief was a friend of one of the board members - it sure felt like it. I never found out. After that tongue lashing and humiliation, I felt lower than dirt itself and made a solemn promise to myself that I'd never allow myself to be disrespected that way again.

In spite of all that, and to my amazement, when all was said and done I was given a one-year release date. A few weeks later I was assigned to work on the outside grounds work crew. Our job was to maintain the facility grounds by mowing, weeding, watering, planting, painting and anything else that needed to be done. After breakfast we'd all meet at the pedestrian gate and wait for the van/bus to pick us up for work at our various locations. At the end of the day we were bused back to our yard.

It was going alright for a while, until we decided to make a batch of pruno (homemade wine). Rule Number Two: If you enjoy a little freedom and job perks, don't get drunk and get caught. We soon discovered we hadn't made enough hooch for everyone and would be a little short.

Back in those days Correctional Staff lived in houses on the institutional property to be close by in case of a riot or other emergency. Which brings me to Rule Number Three: Do not steal from the people who are your overseers – especially their booze! A couple of the work crew decided to break into staff housing and grab some vodka and gin. Oh yeah, we partied to the max … until staff noticed we were having way more fun than usual and had us bused back to the yard. We were so smashed that we didn't care when we were busted and sent to the hole. In the hole, you're in a prison inside the prison and got nothing coming. We were there about a month and lost good jobs. I didn't really care, though. But it was the last time I ever touched alcohol of any kind.

Chapter 4
The Hole
1972

At five o'clock in the morning I was startled awake at the opening of the food tray slot in the door. Breakfast was about to be delivered. The hole, as it's named for administrative segregation (Ad Seg) consists of cells with just a bunk, sink, and toilet. Nothing fancy. My hangover from drinking the day before was still throbbing at my temples. It was cold and unusually quiet. After breakfast, it was all about reading books and waiting for the next meal. Later in the day several of us were allowed into the enclosed and isolated exercise yard for an hour or two of fresh air and sunshine.

One day while on the exercise yard a neighbor in the hole introduced himself as George Jackson. Jackson had been there for a while and we ended up talking many times. I soon discovered he was an educated man, especially in the art of discipline, gang style.

Later on, word was out that Jackson and a group he was hanging with took over the Adjustment Center at San Quentin Prison, which is on the first tier. The Adjustment Center is like a maximum-security lockup hole. Jackson and his group supposedly killed several guards with guns that were smuggled in by his attorney. During the disturbance, knowing he was a marked man, Jackson sacrificed himself for others involved. He was shot and killed by guards for trying to escape (or so they say).

My thirty-day punishment was coming to an end. I went back to committee and my release date was adjusted by eighteen months for disciplinary action. I was returned to the mainline population.

Crackers and I eventually drifted apart and sought out other friends to hang with. He ended up with a more questionable crowd, of sorts. He got rolled up and transferred to Susanville prison up near the Nevada border.

I started hanging with a different caliber of people including a guy named 'Flaco', who I also knew from my CYA years. Flaco was housed with Crackers in Lassen Hall. We were all socializing and trying to pass our time to escape the boredom of everyday prison life – lifting weights, playing chess or just walking laps around the yard. Anything to make the day go by.

I was getting a drink of water at the fountain one afternoon when Lil' Danny from Salinas struck up a conversation with me. I'd met Danny for the first time at Soledad. He asked me if I knew Flaco well. I told him, "Well enough." And asked, why? Lil' Danny informed me that Flaco was very influential and connected with a very bad crowd known as the Mexican Mafia (EME), which is one of the active prison gangs. I didn't mention anything to Lil' Danny at the time about the friendship between Flaco and me.

As other gangs were being established, members of each one needed to be identified as to their affiliation and allegiance. This was accomplished by having a tattoo (tat, or writing) of their gang insignia placed on a specific part of the body. Larry was from Salinas, and a member of the Nuestra Familia (NF). On day, 'Big Albert' from San Francisco, also an NF member, and I were sitting on the grass kicking back and talking, when we were interrupted by Larry, who casually joined in the conversation. After a few minutes, Larry pulled Big Albert aside and asked him if he had his 'writing' on yet. Big Albert told Larry that with all the other tattoos on his body, he didn't have room for one more.

About this time Flaco had noticed some fresh tattoos on other NF members. Flaco, being a friend, approached me during a recruiting period and offered to sponsor me if I wanted to join with his affiliation (EME).

I told him I had other personal projects going on at the time and wasn't interested in joining, but I'd let him know if I changed my mind. Each new member had to be sponsored by a current member to join a gang. The hot summer of '72 was in full swing and the tensions between rival gangs was escalating. The tension was so great it would only take a smirk, a wrong look, or a misunderstood word, for the yard to explode.

And then it happened. A guy named 'Jo-Boy' from the 'Avenues' gang in Los Angeles, and his second in command, Artie, were associates of the EME. The following happened in just a few short minutes. 'Bozo' and 'Lugo' were transferred from Folsom Prison to Soledad to reorganize the NF. At this time both the NF and EME were at war in the prison. Also, the Aryan Brotherhood (AB) and the EME were allies with each other. Both yards had a mix of gang members living together. Jo-Boy and Artie (EME) were on yard-2 along with a lot of other EME members, as were a couple of guys named Charlie and Lil' Albert from Watsonville (NF).

One sunny Sunday morning Charlie snuck over to yard-1 through the back of the kitchens and told Lil' Danny that Lugo just got stabbed in the back by Woody from the AB. Lugo had his heart punctured, and even though he was mortally wounded he had enough strength to go from his cell down the hall to the shower area, where he collapsed in Bozo's arms. Lil' Danny and I were having breakfast when word came down from the Godfathers for Lil' Danny to have Flaco hit in retaliation for Lugo's death. Lil' Danny immediately left me at the table to go take care of business. After chow was over and I was exiting the dining hall, I looked across the yard to Rainier Hall where a crowd had gathered. A group of inmates were pushing a gurney with Flaco on it across the yard to the infirmary.

I saw Flaco with the knife in his chest and knew he was gone. Just then I saw 'Bruiser', a 300-pound guy, and 'Diamond' from Fresno, both NF members, heading for the water fountain on the baseball field to clean up and wash blood off themselves (from killing Flaco). As if what just happened wasn't enough, the NF Godfathers told Flapper (from Stockton) and Lil' Danny to hit two more EME gang members who had come over from yard-2 to see the action. Lil' Danny refused to participate in hitting two EME members, so I volunteered to go with Flapper to do the hit because Flapper was my friend and I didn't want him to go by himself. We were supplied with a couple of knives from the NF members and socks to wash the blood off, in case we got any on us. Because of what was happening on yard-1, tension and anxiety was as high as ever. The two EME gang members saw Flapper and I approaching them and hastily retreated to their own yard via the control gate, never to be seen again. The weapons that were used for the hit on Flaco came from some of the NF members that had gathered at Rainier Hall. They had disappeared into the background through a group of NF members, with the exception of the knife Flaco had in him. You'd be surprised how easily weapons can blend in anywhere and not be discovered.

Both yards were locked down while the investigation was going on. All suspected and known gang members, about sixty in all, from both yards were gathered up and sent to the hole pending investigation and disciplinary action. This was all new to me, as far as being a suspect in gang activity. Needless to say, my anxiety level was high, not knowing what was going to happen. The hole was designed so that a row of cells was facing west, with a wall down the middle separating the east-facing cells and a utility vent in the wall between the cells. The administration decided that for the protection of everyone concerned, it would be best to keep the gangs separated to prevent further bloodshed.

After two days in the hole I noticed that everyone on my side was NF members, and on the other side the EME members were housed. Being all of nineteen years old and new to this gang stuff, I was a little nervous and unsure of myself, not knowing all the do's and don'ts yet. I had mixed emotions about all that had gone on and had no idea what was going to happen next. I had friends on both sides and wasn't officially in any gang yet. After I started talking to some of the EME members through the vent I was quickly reprimanded by one of the NF and told not to communicate with the enemy. I was thinking then that my mind had already been made up, I was going to join the NF gang.

We all knew that emergency transfers to other prisons to break up the groups was going to happen soon. Sure enough, two buses pulled up behind R&R and we were off to our next destination. Our property would be sent at another time. 'Diamond' and 'Bullwinkle' from Sacramento asked me to go with them to Susanville. But I didn't have a choice in the matter. We were told we'd be going to Susanville, but at the last minute, Bozo, Robert, Big Albert, a few others and I were sent to San Quentin. The other NF members: Lil' Bobbie, Larry, Lil' Albert, Lil' Danny, and Bruiser, all ended up being transferred to DVI at Tracy. All the EMEs were sent to Folsom Prison.

I lost track of a lot of those guys and didn't see them for a few years. Bozo and I were seated together for the ride to our new home. Needless to say, my anxiety level jumped when I found out where I was headed, because of all the rumors about San Quentin and everything I'd heard about the horrors behind the walls. Bullwinkle, Fat Mike, Ray and the others were loaded onto another bus and sent to Susanville. Unfortunately, those souls going into Susanville were not as lucky as the rest of us.

Chapter 5
San Quentin Prison
1972

Bozo sat next to me on the bus ride to San Quentin. He knew I was anxious about coming to this prison and helped comfort my fears by telling me he had been there before and knew the program somewhat. It was about three in the afternoon when we arrived. The bus stopped in front of those famous stone guards' towers at the entrance. There's a gift shop of inmate-made handicrafts just outside the prison grounds. The entrance archway gates are made of thick steel bars that were manually opened and closed to let the bus through. After exiting at the rotunda, all our files were reviewed by staff for housing placement. It was decided that we would all go to the hole until we were seen by committee (since we were coming from the hole at Soledad).

We were escorted through the archway under the gun tower on the upper yard, a long fifteen-foot-high wall. As we made our way to the hole, Bozo was giving me a running commentary and a personal tour of the place. He showed me where George Jackson had lived and died. He was real informative. The upper yard was covered with a large sloped roof with catwalks all around. A real eye opener was the fact that everyone on the prison grounds was under the gun twenty-four-seven. There's a maze of catwalks in and surrounding the prison. We made a left turn just past the Adjustment Center (AC) with armed guards keeping a watchful eye the entire time. Then we passed a flight of concrete stairs on the right, leading down to the lower big yard. That yard holds approximately three-to-five-thousand convicts. This lower yard also has most of the support services, e.g., laundry, library, clinic, etc. We then zigzagged around the canteen to the hole just ahead.

We finally arrived at the hole (B-Section) after the scenic walk. The hole has to be the bowels of the prison. It has four sections and is five tiers high. Armed guards pace back and forth on the catwalk positioned across from the barred cell doors, with the outside wall and broken windows as backdrop. B-Section is ugly and filthy and the place reeks with an assortment of repulsive odors. Most of the foul smells come from birds, cats, and rats that have also made B-Section their home. There must not have been anything such as animal rodent control in those days. Just one big noisy, nasty, smelly family.

As we entered B-Section, the first tier was a row of cells known as strip cells, which are cells within cells and were used as further disciplinary action for incorrigible types who won't program/behave. The first door is solid and locked. The second door is a barred door with nothing at all in the cell.

The second tier inmates were all NF members, with the exception of me. All of the AB's and EME's were on the third tier. There are a hundred cells per tier, that I know of. Each cell is four-feet wide by nine-feet long. One man cells only. When I laid flat on my bed my hand could touch the opposite wall. There's a bed, toilet, and a sink. That's it. What you might call a no frills flat. The door locking device is called a front bar/back bar system. Each bar releases fifty cells in a row at a time.

Communication in the hole between inmates is a well-established 'fishing' system. A long string (line) is wrapped around a small paperback book for weight, with a 'kite' (note) attached to the book. When the weight gets to the destination the receiver snags the line and pulls it into his cell. Message delivered It's primitive, but it works.

A couple of hours after I settled into my temporary home a line landed in front of the cell with a kite attached. It was from 'DR' (Death Row Joe), asking me questions about where I came from and why I was at San Quentin. I filled him in on the details and satisfied his curiosity.

About a week later I went to committee. Lil' Albert and I were the only two approved for the mainline (GP) General Population. Before leaving, word came down for me to watch Lil' Albert's back. Within a day we were both sent to East Block, third tier, where Albert and I were next door neighbors

East Block was not much different from B-Section, except that East Block has a warehouse configuration where inmates have two possible views. One overlooks the yard, the other is of the bayside. Back in the day there were no TV's or radios to help take your mind off boring or more destructive thoughts. Books were available for those who could read. By three in the afternoon program was over.

Everyone was in their cells except for one inmate known as a "Key Monitor." A Key Monitor was a trustee/runner who carried a set of keys to everybody's cell for that section. I was really surprised that an inmate was allowed such access to cells, especially considering the security concerns of other inmates. But the Key Monitor was under constant supervision by armed guards on the catwalks. He was also the only inmate allowed to climb vertically between the tiers instead of using the stairs. His 'play' (hustle) was to sell burritos and sandwiches from leftover food from the chow hall for a buck each. He'd deliver notes, books and other materials requested by staff or inmates.

After breakfast the next morning, Albert and I went to the yard. I started getting weird vibes. I noticed other people seemed to be staying clear of us, like we were lepers or something. Albert must have picked up on it too, he told me to stay clear and that he'd be back in a few minutes. After about twenty minutes he returned. I asked him where he'd gone and he told me he'd gone to see a guy named 'Rebel'.

Rebel was from Maravilla, which is a gang from East Los Angeles which at the time was allied with the NF. We continued to walk the yard and I again asked Albert if he was NF. Again, he replied, 'No' and asked me why I was asking. I told him about the message I had received in the hole about watching his back. Albert didn't seem too surprised when I told him this. Otherwise, the day was uneventful.

The next day I noticed Rebel at Albert's door talking in hushed tones. After Rebel left I asked Albert what was going on. He told me that what he was going to divulge to me was to stay between us in the strictest confidence. He then told me that, in fact, he was an NF member, that he was to make a hit, and that Rebel was his connection for a knife and had told him who the target was. The target was an AB named 'Animal' who lived about three doors down from us. I told Albert I was upset for him lying to me and for not allowing me time to get a knife. He told me not to worry, because Rebel was to bring him a knife later in the evening.

That night after chow, Albert did get a knife. Everybody knew that after arriving at San Quentin, if you could last five days on the yard without anything adverse happening, you would be cleared to go about your business. And our five days (to make a hit or be hit) was about up. It's called prison politics.

The next morning was the fourth day on the yard and we knew something had to be done. The only problem was, we couldn't find the target. The rest of the day was normal, under the circumstances, so we parted ways for the time-being.

About three in the afternoon I noticed an individual known as 'Snake', an American Indian, talking to Albert in a quiet way, but I didn't think anything of it at the time. After afternoon count cleared we went to dinner and I reminded Albert we had to act and make a hit. Albert informed me that he had given the knife to Snake because Snake had told him Rebel had made a mistake and wasn't supposed to have given the knife to him. I was upset and told Albert so, and said that he shouldn't have given the knife back to Snake. After I spoke my mind, I let it go. We returned to our cells for the rest of the evening.

The next morning was day five and we went to breakfast. We made our plans to go to yard that morning, Albert was going to the sweat lodge later. As we headed back to East Block and the rotunda area, I sensed something wasn't right and stopped at the door. Albert told me to stay there in the rotunda, that he had to see someone on the fifth tier on the yard side of the building. Within a few moments, I heard a commotion coming from the third tier. As I approached the first tier, Albert came running toward me holding his right side, yelling, "I've been hit!" He fell into my arms, bleeding ... he'd been stabbed. I asked him what he was doing on the third tier instead of the fifth. He told me that he had changed his mind and was heading back to the cell.

I asked him who did it and with labored breathing he told me, "It was Animal." Animal just happened to be the target that Albert was looking for, it looked as if he found him. Later we learned that Snake was an AB, not an NF as Albert was led to believe. Animal and Snake were in the same gang.

I knew I had to get out of the vicinity and get cleaned up. One thing you never want to do is get caught with blood of any kind on yourself or your clothes, and I looked as if I'd just left the butcher shop. Well, that didn't pan out. Staff noticed me and all the blood, cuffed me up and took me to the hole pending investigation on the stabbing. Albert survived his wounds and a few hours later, with a few stitches and his side patched up, he was also taken to the hole.

Kites were flying back and forth between cells with everybody trying to get the 411 on what happened. Albert sent me a kite asking me not to say anything to anybody about what happened and said he'd take care of it. It really wasn't any of my business anyway.

After about a week the primary investigation cleared Albert and me. We were both allowed to go out to the B-Section exercise yard, which consisted of a handball and basketball court facing the bay.

I was on the tier that housed NF members, and I went to the NF yard. Some NF members I didn't know came up to me to introduce themselves and to welcome me. They were: DR, Joker, Robert. Bozo, Buggy and Charlie (who were brothers of Babo). Albert was also on the yard. Joker was very likeable and had some history behind him. He was the clown of the second tier in B-Section and helped break the tension when needed. Joker was also known for his drawing of the NF symbol - the 'Knife Through the Hat' still used today. He was also the boxing heavyweight champ back in the 60s, and full of talent.

Robert came over to me and informed me that he had to go to a meeting and that I was not allowed to attend because I wasn't a member. I could see that Albert was the topic of the meeting because he was getting a tongue-lashing from the others, presumably for his near-fatal mistake.

After about a half hour the meeting broke up. At that time, DR came over to me and was making small talk. I could tell he was interrogating me about what had happened to Albert. Remembering what Albert told me, I told DR that I didn't know anything about Albert's activities leading up to the stabbing. A couple of nights later, the third tier where the EMEs and ABs lived was noisy with laughter and joking around, a name or two were tossed into the conversation and a loud cheer erupted. Robert sent me a kite informing me that two NF members, Diamond and Bullwinkle, had been killed at Susanville a few days earlier. The information was confirmed by a newspaper article. It was a shock to hear this about guys I knew, guys I considered friends.

That night I reminisced about the good times I had with them, which stirred up a lot of anger at their passing. Later, information about what really happened to Diamond and Bullwinkle trickled down. Word had it that they were housed in Dorm 39 at Susanville, with four NF living in the same dorm. At night, the four NF would take turns standing watch. Two would sleep while the other two stood sentry. Bullwinkle was sleeping in his bunk and Diamond was in the shower. Fat Mike saw two EMEs coming toward the dorm, but instead of alerting the others of potential danger, he split and, like the coward he was, hid behind some blacks. Ray was unaware of what was coming.

The first EME, Sleepy, went over to Bullwinkle and started stabbing him with such viciousness that Bullwinkle was completely decapitated, with the exception of a vein holding him together. The other EME, Pelon, went to the shower area where Diamond was completely unaware of what was going on. Pelon got the jump on him and stabbed Diamond repeatedly in the upper torso. Ray heard the commotion, grabbed a large trashcan and started slamming it on Pelon to try and get him off Diamond. Pelon's adrenaline was pumping though and he just shrugged off the counter-assault, continuing to stab

Diamond. At that point, Ray panicked and ran off, leaving Diamond to his demise. Ray's actions were considered among the NF to be an act of cowardice.

Diamond later died from his injuries, even after being taken by Life-flight to the nearest hospital. After the dust settled, Ray testified to the murders of Bullwinkle and Diamond. Sleepy and Pelon were found guilty and given life sentences. A couple of months later Pelon committed suicide because he didn't want to do the time. Sleepy is still in a California prison.

The next day word came down through the grapevine that an NF member by the name of Woodchuck was transferred from San Quentin to Tehachapi Prison. As soon as he arrived there he was stabbed and killed. He wasn't even out of his transportation jumpsuit when they got to him. Because of the murder of Woodchuck and the deaths of Bullwinkle and Diamond, retaliation was in order.

Back at Soledad Prison, during the ways of the Godfathers, the gangs could intermingle with each other without such adverse action like going to war.

A relative newcomer to the system, and an NF member, named Cisco was targeted by the EME to be hit because he was trying to get something for nothing. Cisco had a drug habit, which is taboo for NF members if you get caught. Cisco just wasn't thinking. The EME lured him to a cell for a fix, and just as he was putting the needle in his arm he looked up to see a guy coming down on him with a knife. It struck him between the shoulder blades. Cisco collapsed right there, and the EME made another hit. If the EME hadn't got to him first the NF would have because of the drug use.

By that time, two other NF members, Chief and Junior, were given the task of hitting two EMEs. During a movie night in the gym at Soledad Central two EMEs saw their last cartoon. The bodies were discovered when the lights came back on. The assailants had disappeared.

Other things were going on that I was completely unaware of. I was making enemies just because I was on the NF tier. I had friends in both gangs, but I had no idea of the gravity of the situation. I was young and naïve, and the politics of the situation were confusing and not easy to accept. Questions rolled through my mind: why were all these guys getting killed, and why was I not made aware of the conflicts and issues that intertwined with the politics between both these gangs?

Robert explained to me that at one time the EME had been known to pressure new Mexicans that were coming into prison. If you weren't with them you were subject to be pressured into drug use, sex, or other adverse acts for EME's purposes. Looking back on the way things were, the majority of Mexicans were from Southern California. The NF didn't believe in this kind of treatment for those of their own culture. The NF also believed in letting people do their own thing. They didn't pressure people to join the NF. There was one rule the NF maintained: when and if you accepted as an NF, no matter where you came from or what ethnic group you were a part of, you were family for life. That meant loyalty above and beyond homeboys, personal friends, and even family. NF came first.

If you were ordered to kill your own brother, sister, mother or father, this order must be carried out for the "Family" without question. It sounds harsh, but that was the way it was in those days. It was called survival. An NF member lived and died only for the purpose of the "Familia".

Two or three weeks later, due to committee action, and because the captain at San Quentin thought I was too young to be housed there, I was put up for transfer to DVI, Tracy. DVI was for CYA rejects and had a reputation as a gladiator school. I knew when I got to DVI I would know a lot of guys from CYA and Soledad North. Because of that I had a lot of anxiety about going there. I tried to nix the transfer, but no luck.

A new constitution had been drawn up that would include all families uniting together under one leader from all the prisons throughout the state. As time went on, DR and I got to be friends. He asked me if I knew of a way to get some information to Folsom Prison. I told him

I got visits from a girlfriend occasionally and she might be able to help.

DR needed to get a message to Babo through my visitor. The message was that Babo was to be the General of NF under the new constitution. With a new chain of command came a new First Captain under the new general.

Until then it was a toss-up between a member named Diata and DR as to who would be the First Captain under the new General. Diata had an edge on DR because Diata had made a kill for the NF and DR had not. Diata had come from a gang called Familia Cinco (Family Five) that was created at California Men's Colony (CMC) at San Luis Obispo in the 1970s. Diata later dropped out of the FC to become an NF member.

Even though a lot of members wanted Diata to be the First Captain, he didn't want the position. One point in DR's favor was the fact that he wrote the new constitution. About two weeks later Babo sent word through my visitor that DR would in fact be the First Captain.

Under the new constitution, the First Captain would be assigned the duties of Head of Security over all NF activities throughout the state. As time progressed, DR asked me if I wanted to join the NF. I was having a lot of conflicting emotions and thoughts about that kind of lifestyle at the time. I told him I wasn't interested.

After committee recommendations for the DVI transfer, and while I was waiting to go, DR asked me if I would be willing to take the constitution and a hit list down to DVI when I went. I didn't have any problem with the request and I told him I would. I stayed up all night copying the new constitution and the hit list. I was to give all this information to an NF member called Peanut, from Stockton, and pass on the message that he would be a captain at DVI.

I asked Robert what DVI was like at Tracy because of all the rumors I had heard. Robert said I would have nothing to worry about, and then he explained.... About two months prior, Bozo from San Jose was hit and killed while watching a show in the TV room. Mike, (Poyo) from

Oakland, my cousin, was with him at the time. Mike ran and didn't render aid when Bozo needed it. So much for Mike's membership.

A week later Huero from San Diego was hit and killed in the kitchen by some EME members. A few days later another NF, Bo, had an attempt on his life when an AB hit him in the head with a pipe. The intention was to bring Bo down, but he shook it off and fought back with a vengeance. Another EME member slowed Bo down by stabbing him in the chest, puncturing a lung. Bo survived to live another day. Huero from Ontario was in charge at DVI and was soon to be released to go home. He had no intention of screwing up his release date, or worse, get killed. Peanut, however, was irate about what was happening to the NF members so he took Huero's position as leader and declared war on the EME at Tracy. Staff was expecting all hell to break loose at any time. The tension was heavy in the air, and when it happened… bloodshed was everywhere.

Exact numbers of casualties were not known but there were a lot of injuries due to stabs, slashes, and broken bones. A lot of pride was hurt. Peanut had constructed a flawless plan to annihilate the EME and any sympathizers, including the ABs, and erase them from the population. Word had it that Peanut's plan was executed all over DVI with such precision that it would make any General proud of his men. The NF cleaned house in one day and earned respect for the NF at the same time. The war was known as the Pearl Harbor of DVI. It's said that no EME would ever walk that line again as long as the NF were there.

Chapter 6
DVI, Tracy, CA
Winter 1972

A few days later I was told to transpack (pack up my property for R&R) to be transported to DVI. Sometime during the evening DR sent me a kite asking if things, meaning the constitution and the hit list, had been put away. I let him know that everything was neatly packed away and not to worry. DR sent me an envelope that contained three items: a Band-aid, a medallion of Saint Christopher, and a note. The note read "If one doesn't work, the other will. Good luck." The meaning was clear.

The following morning about three o'clock several other inmates and I were waking up for pre-trip preparations by transport officers. It seemed to me that every time I get transferred it was cold and rainy outside. We boarded the bus for the two-hour ride. After a year in one place, it would be nice for a change. The bus pulled out into traffic and we headed for Tracy. I had time to think on the trip. We passed my home town and memories came to mind about family and childhood days. I was homesick and I only had nine months to go to get to the house. The thought stirred up a little bit of excitement in me. A lot can happen in nine months, though.

A little history on DVI (Deuel Vocational Institute). It was opened in the 1950s and at first the California Youth Authority operated it as a facility for incorrigible youth. Years later the Adult Corrections Department took over its operation. It had an Olympic-size swimming pool, tennis courts, basketball courts, etc. The food was very good there; you were served generous portions and a nice variety. In the early years when the prisons were built, three of them were built using the same blueprint. They were Soledad, Vacaville, and DVI at Tracy. This came to light when the bus approached DVI. It looked exactly like Soledad Central.

The bus pulled all the way to the back of the prison to the sally port for entrance to R&R. As soon as I got there I noticed one thing that really stood out - the NF were more organized. Word from one prison to another gets there before you do.

When I got off the bus, two members from the NF, Danny and Lil' Bobby from Salinas, both of whom I had known at Soledad North, were there to greet me. I was impressed. I spent two hours at R&R before being escorted, with five other inmates, by staff and two NF members (just for me). We went to the hole at K-Wing until we were assigned permanent housing at committee.

When we were escorted to the hole Danny told me to contact Snake from Bakersfield. I went to the first tier in the hole. It was smelly, loud, dark, and had single-cells with barred doors. There are two sides to the hole, the left side and right side. I ended up on the right side about eight cells down. I didn't know it until later, but Snake was on the left side. I got settled in and waited for someone to contact me.

Nothing. No contact from anyone. A few minutes later two white guys walked by with towels wrapped around their bodies. I received two very ugly stares. The both unwrapped their towels to expose large lettered "AB" tats. Oops, my bad! I immediately backed away from the bars, a few shades paler from the shock. This taught me a valuable lesson: Don't ask, and be patient.

After my blunder, I got a call through the vent from a cell on the other side. It was Snake. He told me to stay away from the bars. I said he didn't have to worry about that since my encounter with the ABs. The next day the C.O. came by and asked if I was NF. I told him no. Then he asked if I wanted to be moved to the other side, to which I replied with a relieved, YES! The day after, I was moved.

A few days later I went to committee and was informed that I'd be assigned to F-wing. However, F-wing didn't have any room available. I'd be temporarily housed in C-wing. F-wing is a pre-release wing for short-timers, inmates with less than a year left before parole. Since I had only nine months left, that's where I would be housed.

It was about seven in the morning when I was relocated to the third tier in C-wing. The first thing I noticed was the cells were facing each other with a walkway running between. That night I met Bo for the first time. He came over and introduced himself and informed me that he lived across from me.

I then asked him where Peanut was because I had some paperwork for him. I was told to hold onto it until the next day when someone would come to pick it up. Bo asked me if I knew Larry from Salinas, and I acknowledged that I did. Bo passed onto me that Larry sends his regards. He mentioned that Larry lived in another wing. That evening I unpacked and stored my property in the locker. I'm glad I travel light. Moving from one prison to another can be unsettling if you have a lot of property. Back in those days we didn't have TVs, radios, and extra baggage. Just the bare minimum. After looking out the window for a few minutes it was time to relax and call it a day. I slept soundly all night.

The next morning after breakfast I went out to the yard and deeply inhaled the fresh morning air. I walked around the yard for a while and happened to run into Larry, Lil' Danny, and few other NF members I knew from the past. It was almost like a family reunion. We embraced and talked about where the other people we've known might be. Some of the members had taken on new names for themselves, gangster names like Frank Nitty, Legs Diamond, Capone, and The Enforcer. This was all part of the new movement about to happen.

I mentioned to Larry that I had paperwork for Peanut. He told me to hang onto it and that it would be picked up later. That evening after dinner, Legs Diamond came by to get the constitution and the hit list for Peanut. For the next few days I was just getting settled in, getting used to the new place and new faces. Every prison is a little different from others in some aspect. Things were going well. Larry and I were walking around one afternoon and he asked me if I wanted to join the

NF. I told him I wasn't interested and the subject was changed. Larry then told me of a new arrival on my tier. He warned me to be careful because the new arrival was an AB who was transferred from Chino Prison for stabbing an NF member. Larry told me to stay away from him, and to stay with Bo when we were outside of our cells.

As I got to know Bo we became friends. He was short in stature, but stout and he could hold his own. The following weekend Bo introduced me to Peanut on the yard. A while later Bo was asked to make a hit on an AB member. I noticed a slight change in his demeanor after that. He seemed distant and I asked him what was on his mind. He had accepted the challenge of making the hit with pleasure, and he told me that he was okay. After seeing who his target was, a white boy about 6-foot-two and well built, it was no wonder why Bo was a little distant. He was mentally gearing up for the hit. It was like comparing David and Goliath. I asked Bo if he needed some back up and he told me 'No', that this was family business and not to worry about it. He told me to stay clear.

That was before we found out that this AB named 'Trashman' was recruiting two others for his group. Larry told us he didn't think the other two guys would get involved and to stay focused on the enemy.

I had a talk with Larry about backing Bo up with his hit. Larry told me he didn't have a problem with this, if it was what I wanted to do. He would set it up to acquire the shanks (homemade knives) for the hit the next day on the yard. The next morning, we picked up the weapons behind the bleachers. Mine was about 12 inches long with a handle. Bo's weapon was a piece of sharpened metal about six inches long with a handle made of wrapped material. They were both made to do deadly damage. I put my knife in my waistband, while Bo put his in his pocket.

Back in the day, before cameras and extra guards, there were blind spots on the yard – areas that were not entirely visible by staff at all times. One of these particular areas was called Dead Man's Alley. It was a walkway with an overhang that runs the length of the gym and leads to the swimming pool. A ruse is played out where an unsuspecting target is lured into Dead Man's Alley, only to never walk out again.

As Bo and I were heading toward this area, we stopped at the water fountain where Larry was standing. All of a sudden, Bo dropped his knife with such a loud metallic, ringing sound that it caught the attention of everyone within hearing distance, including Trashman and his two prospective associates. As quickly as humanly possible, I slid my foot over the knife to keep others from seeing it. I played it off by looking in another direction. So much for best laid plans. At the sound of the knife dropping to the ground, Trashman and his two associates spotted us at the water fountain and immediately took off running in the opposite direction. Staff knew something was going on, or about to happen, but they didn't get involved. Due to Bo's blunder and the target fleeting, Larry told us that the hit was going to have to be made in the gym that night. He also warned us to be careful at evening chow and for us to go together, which we did. We saw Trashman and his buddies in the dining room. But they were acting as if they didn't have a care in the world, or maybe that's what they wanted us to think.

The meal that evening was hamburgers, French fries, cole slaw, iced tea, and Jell-O. After the meal, we returned to our cells until the PM yard release, when we would go to the gym. I noticed that Bo didn't come out at all. I thought maybe he'd gone ahead without me. On my way out, I picked up my knife and stuck it in my waistband, then headed for the gym.

When I got there, a few NF members approached me. We walked around the gym until we saw Larry. He asked me where Bo was. I replied, "I don't know, I thought he was already here." Then we saw Trashman and his two associates enter the gym. We knew that the hit was going to have to go down, but Bo was nowhere to be found. Larry asked me if I'd brought my blade, and I told him that I had it on me. Larry then told me that because Bo wasn't there a hold would have to be put on the hit.

I told Larry, "Hell no! I'll do it myself!" I then took the knife from my waistband and put it in my pocket for easy access. That's when I learned why sheaths were made. As I put the twelve-inch knife into my pocket, I was totally unaware that the blade had cut through the bottom of my pocket and neatly slit open my pants leg. The blade was sticking out in plain view for anybody and everybody looking. The only thing that kept it from coming all the way through was the handle. As we were walking away, Trashman and his compadres saw the thing sticking out of my pants and took off running out of the gym, leaving me wondering what the hell had spooked them.

When my blunder was pointed out to me, I looked down to see that long blade sticking out of my pants in front of God and everybody. My face turned three shades redder than ever before. I immediately pulled it out and put it back in my waistband. Larry called off the hit for another day

The gym closed at nine that evening and we all went back to our cells. I saw Bo but didn't get a chance to talk with him. That night I sat on my bunk and thought about my upcoming parole date. I was also thinking that I wished Trashman would lock it up, or at least break a toe and go to the hospital so I wouldn't have to do this hit. As I thought about it I fell asleep.

The smell of breakfast drifted through the wing and woke me up to the start of a brand new day. I stopped by Bo's cell and picked him up on the way to breakfast. I asked him why he didn't come the night before. He explained that he got locked in and that's why he didn't make it to the gym. Meanwhile, Larry wanted to see us as soon as the yard opened after breakfast.

I told Bo what took place the evening before. He said he was sorry for not being there, but couldn't help but smirk after hearing the whole story of the exposed blade fiasco. After breakfast, we went back to our cells to freshen up and wait for the eight A.M. yard release. We didn't carry our knives with us to the yard though. Bo and I met Larry at the bleachers and he informed us that the hit would have to be made that night in the TV room. He said that Trashman had to know we were up to something, and that fact made him a threat. I told Larry that there was no way to make the hit in the TV room because staff searched us going in. He asked me if there was any way to get the weapons into the TV room. I told him that maybe the porter could help. He was a guy named Chino that I knew from CYA, and I believed I could trust him. I'd ask him to put the knives in the TV room before release so they would be there before we arrived. Larry was okay with that, but I'd have to talk with Chino first.

That afternoon I found Chino and explained the situation. He said that he didn't want to get involved. I explained that he wouldn't be involved, that all he had to do was wrap the knives in paper and leave them under the first bench near the TV. We would take it from there. Chino finally agreed after I assured him that he was otherwise left out of it. Everything was set, the plan was in motion, the trap laid.

Chapter 7
The Hit
December 1972

That night at TV room release, Bo and I came out of our cells on the third tier and headed down to the bottom tier. Each wing has a TV room on the first tier allowing approximately 50 convicts to watch while sitting on the benches or standing around. Trashman and his associates didn't come out. As we were coming down the stairs I saw Chino standing off to the side. He gave me a nod, indicating the weapons were in place. As we got to the TV room, staff were doing pat-down searches before anybody was allowed in. As Bo and I entered, he went to the right and I circled around to left, down the aisles with the benches between us. At the first bench near the TV, we found the knives exactly where Chino had put them. We picked them up and went to the third row and sat down.

Another NF member, 'Mac', was standing up in the left side corner reading a paper. From his vantage point at the rear of the TV room he could see through the windows into the hallway. He was the point man and lookout. After a while, Trashman and his two partners entered the TV room. They sat down two rows behind us. About an hour into the program, Bo said, "Let's do this." He got up and walked to the bench behind them. I got up and went up the left aisle, circled back and stopped at the end of the bench where Trashman was sitting, facing him. In an instant, the three of them jumped up into a fighting stance. The associates leaped over the benches and attacked Bo. Trashman lunged at me just as I was charging him. I stabbed him a bunch of times, as fast as I could move. It seemed like forever that the scuffle went on. The two associates moved from Bo and headed towards Mac in the corner. Everything was happening in a blur, but time seemed to stand still.

Bo managed to get to his feet and he went after Trashman, stabbing him and wrestling with him. Trashman was still fighting back, holding his ground, but he was leaking bad. I ran over to the window, as planned, and tossed my knife out. Then I moved to the other side of the TV room to blend in with the crowd. Bo and Trashman were still going at it, so I ran back to them to try and help Bo so he could get rid of his knife.

Trashman was starting to slow down, feeling the effects of the loss of blood and exhaustion. He pulled back, giving me time and opportunity to help Bo toss his knife out the window on the yard side.

After the knives were disposed of we've moved back into the crowd trying to blend in with the rest of the inmates. Mac was lying down, semiconscious from the beating he took from the two associates. The guards were alerted and started breaking windows with block-guns (a combination device about 12 inches long, about the size of a flashlight, that's used as a Billy-club and also fires teargas).

The windows in the TV room were about 5 feet up from the floor and run the length of the room. I crouched down under the windows and headed towards Mac. Glass was breaking all around. I grabbed him and dragged him back to where the crowd was watching the action, trying to blend in. I noticed a BGF (Black Guerilla Family) member named Junebug sitting on the bench near the TV, taking in the real-life action entertainment. He brought it to my attention that my shirt was almost completely soaked in blood.

Staff pounced on Trashman and his associates as they were trying to flee the room. I had to get rid of the shirt, but I didn't have a spare one, and I had to have one in order to get out of there. Junebug had two shirts on, a white T-shirt and his blue one. He tossed me the blue one as I tore the blood-stained shirt off and threw it to the side.

The TV room was closed down for investigation and staff patted us down on the way out. We were ordered back to our cells, and when I got there I washed up to rid myself of any blood evidence. I was in there about 20 minutes and laid down on my bunk to recuperate. I thought I gotten away with it, then staff showed up for a more thorough examination. They looked me over head to toe and found a small amount of blood on the tattoo on my right wrist. I'd somehow missed it while washing up. It was a dead giveaway!

The officer took a photograph of my wrist with the blood spots on it, handcuffed me, and took me to the hole. I was on the second tier of K-wing, second from the end. About 10 minutes later, Bo was escorted into the hole and shown to his cell. Meanwhile, Mac had been taken to the hospital due to the beating he taken from the two associates. He was later brought to the hole, and the two associates were brought in as well. They were housed on the third tier.

Around midnight, staff pulled Bo, me, and Mac out and escorted us downstairs to a room where we were read our rights. We were told that Trashman had died from his injuries and all three of us were being charged with his murder. We all refused to talk about what had happened and were returned to our cells. The next day I met my neighbor, Casper from Salinas. At one time the cells had been double-bunked, but for safety reasons the top bunks were removed. That left small holes in the wall where the mounting bolts had been where we could communicate with our neighbors using the holes.

Casper introduced me to Sharky from Salinas. He was in the cell on the other side of me. Casper warned me to be careful when on the tier and gave me the rundown on how the program worked. A guy named 'Ninney', who was housed mid-tier, kept a knife stashed for emergencies. We were allowed out of our cells for 25 minutes a day for exercise, but there was a catch. The tier was full of mixed gang members from AB, BGF, EME, NF, and a bunch of other unknown gangs that might be trying to make a name for themselves. Only four cells were popped open at a time for exercise, and you never knew who was coming out or who might be a threat!

Casper said that as soon as I was released from the cell to run down to Ninney's cell and pick up the knife. That way at least I would have a chance at survival in case anybody got stupid and went for me.

Each tier in the hole has a double-wide catwalk with a ceiling-to-floor fence extending down the middle to separate the staff from the convicts. This is to allow staff to monitor inside the cells without putting themselves in harm's way with convicts who might have weapons.

Two weeks later, at about nine in the morning the officer popped four cells open. One of the four was a known EME, and another cell held an NF member named Gary from San Diego. Gary was half white and half Mexican. During that time, it was common to release opposing gang members. It happened all the time, just about every day. Gary was 6-footer and 220 pounds of brawn. He had a definite advantage over his opponent. Taking no chances, when his cell door opened, Gary ran down to Ninney's cell, grabbed the knife, then waited in the middle of the tier facing the EME member to see what he was going to do.

The EME headed for his homeboy's cell, who held a knife for the EME's. Without hesitation, he immediately lunged at Gary. But, with Gary's longer arms and quick reactions, he drew first blood and continued to stab the EME guy until staff arrived and chased Gary off with tear gas from their bat-guns. Gary headed to Ninney's cell and handed the knife off. Ninney flushed it down the toilet to lose the evidence.

Tier staff ordered Gary to approach the barred gate to be handcuffed so they could enter the fenced-in tier and render aid to the downed EME member. He complied. Gary had to have his eyes flushed out because of the tear gas irritation, and was photographed with blood all over him. He was checked for injuries and two hours later returned to his cell in the hole. The EME member survived his wounds, was photographed, patched up, and placed in a cell on the opposite side of the tier.

The administration knew about the gangs being at war but didn't take any steps to prevent violence up to that point. The rest of the day the tier was closed down for cleanup, and stayed closed for two more days, pending investigation of the incident.

Ninney ran the tier I was on, even though he held no rank. He, along with other tier leaders, were gathered up and escorted to the committee room where the Facility Program Administrator (PA) was waiting. The tier leaders were informed by the PA that because of the violence between the gangs, there would be no program until moves were made to separate them by tier.

After this announcement, there were no questions, comments, or complaints from anyone. When Ninney returned from the PA meeting he sent kites to all the NF members, including me, because I was considered an NF sympathizer, as to what the plans were going to be for the next couple of days.

The rest of the week gang members were shifted to tiers of their own affiliation, or with allies of their group. NF members that I knew came over from the other two tiers to ours on the second tier. There was Lil' Albert who I knew from San Quentin, Snake from Bakers, Oso from San Jose. After everyone was moved, one side of K-wing (on the second tier) was used for housing NF and BGF members. The first tier was for new arrivals and overflow from the second tier.

The same thing was happening on the opposite side with the EMEs and ABs, who were allies. There were still a few other convicts who had no known affiliation with any gangs, and who were always being watched with a suspicious eye from other members on the tier.

Program was slowly being allowed back, a little at a time, in order to see how everybody was adjusting. No new problems. Everybody was doing okay. I was talking with Sharky one afternoon and he asked me why I hadn't joined NF yet. I told him Larry had already asked to be my sponsor when I was ready to join. In my own mind, I was beginning to see that I could be useful to the family (Nuestra Familia). I had noticed that the tier I was on needed organization. One day

Ninney and I got together, and I explained everything to him as to why I hadn't joined the NF before this. I also told him that I needed to get word to Larry. The time had come; I was ready to commit my allegiance to the NF as a sworn member.

Chapter 8
March 1973

A few days later, on March 15, 1973, confirmation was received from Larry that I had been approved to join the NF. On this date, I was officially "Married" into the Nuestra Familia, which is a lifetime commitment - until the day I die.

A month later an incident occurred that caused Peanut to be sent to the hole in K-wing. Now we had a captain in the hole, with Ninny as a First Lieutenant for all of K-Wing. Just when we thought things were starting to settle down a little, word came down the pike that Babo, the NF General, had just arrived at the hole and was housed directly underneath me on the first tier. Babo was at Folsom last I'd heard, and there was no reason given as to why he was here at DVI.

Communication on a tier was never a problem. A message could be sent by kite, in person, or just by yelling. Communications between upper and lower tiers took a lot more ingenuity and finesse. One of the ways was to completely purge all the water out of the toilet bowls of both upper and lower toilets of cells directly above and below one another. This allowed a direct line of communication through the sewer system. But there is a gross factor involved. If you need to communicate in this manner, in order to make it effective, you have to put a towel over your head while sticking your face right down into the bowl. And the other person, likewise.

The only problem with this procedure, other than the repulsive stench, is that the enemy can do the same and eavesdrop on the conversation. It has to be very brief. Another way to pass a kite is to tie a bar of soap to a piece of sheet string (with a note attached) and flush it down to the lower tier toilet. The receiver also flushes a line with soap attached, the lines tangle and the receiver pulls it in. Message received. All messages must be approved by the tier Lieutenant before the General receives it.

Chapter 9
The Snitch

After a week of communicating with the General, he was approved for Mainline. The next morning I knew it was going to be one of those days. My cell was having plumbing problems and was deemed unsanitary to live in, so I was forced to move to another cell. They moved me to the first cell on the first tier right next to the barred gate. My new neighbor was a BGF named Leonard.

Mac was four cells down from me. Since the three of us had been in the hole Mac had been spending more time out of his cell than in. He was going to the doctor a lot, which I personally didn't find suspicious considering the beating he took in the TV room. Leonard, however, brought it to my attention that he might be snitching Bo and I off. I wasn't really worried about it. Mac was a loyal NF member and Bo trusted him. One night I asked Mac why he was leaving the tier so much and he told me it was because he was still getting medical treatment, which I halfway accepted. Then, one day he went out for a doctor's appointment and didn't come back. That sent up a big red flag.

The following week the Assistant District Attorney came by and officially informed Bo and I that we were being charged with Trashman's death. When this happened, we knew for sure that Mac had turned state's evidence against us.

The day was over and the night was closing in. The tier gets mighty quiet with no radios or TV's. It's peaceful. But lately that hadn't always been the case. Some of my nights over the past few months had been anything but peaceful. I was waking up with nightmares, my heart pounding, sweat running out of me like I was a sprinkler. I learned later that this is classic Post Traumatic Stress Syndrome, and usually caused by a past traumatic event. In my case I think it had more to do with what the future might bring, and worrying about that. I had a lot of anxiety and fear about the possibility of being killed or maimed for life. Remember, I was still just a youngster. A lot was being thrown at me all at once. The one good thing about fear is it kept me very alert to my surroundings, almost to the point of paranoia. Which brings me to my next subject, discipline.

Chapter 10
Schooling, K-Wing
1973

While in the hole our time was spent purposefully. Ninney told us that all NF members were required to be schooled and trained in the ways of survival and warfare. In order to do that we had to study the NF Constitution and memorize the Articles of the Constitution, and know them inside and out, backward and forward. Hand-to-hand combat training was a must, as was the most effective ways to manufacture and use weapons. You had to know how to grab an enemy by his shirt and pull him toward you while thrusting a knife four inches into his chest and piercing his heart muscle. You had to know where all the major arteries are to be able to cause the maximum damage in the shortest time. There are slashing and stabbing techniques, and methods of accomplishing varying degrees of damage. Sometimes you're not trying to kill an opponent, other times it's him or you. You need to know how to fend off attacks, and be able to battle multiple assailants in a wide range of scenarios. There was a punching bag on the tier for practice. We also learned about making zip guns, knives, and metal bullets. Most of it was about loyalty, discipline, and taking orders without question.

The only books you get in the hole are those your family sends in from the streets. Some books are specifically requested; books on the ways of the Italian mafia were valued. That way we were able to see how they organized and operated, and we learned what mistakes they made in order to avoid them ourselves. It was important that we operated as a team and a family, and grow the NF to be something to be respected. It was a challenge to do the schooling every day. We only had about 20 minutes for showers and outside the cell time. There was no such thing as idle time in the hole.

In 1973 a trial started down in Chino, and myself and an NF member from each prison were called as witnesses. The trial had a two-fold purpose. One was the actual trial itself, and the other was to get us together for the NF reorganization so we could go over details and get our plans coordinated. What better way to be able to get us all together than to be called as witnesses?

Because Bo and I were also due in court for the murder of Trashman, it meant I wouldn't be able to attend the meeting at Chino and participate in the future planning of the new Nuestra Familia. I would have to wait and hear what went down.

The head of the EME, and an early founder of the gang, was a very intelligent and popular individual. His name was Cheyenne from Bakersfield; he was considered an elder because of his experience and time as an EME member. Cheyenne was a person that was highly thought of and easy to talk to. Many consider him to have been someone who was very much ahead of his time.

During the time of the Black Panthers, back in the 60s, a Latino group called the "Brown Berets" was born, and chapters were initiated throughout a few California cities. Cheyenne and I both came from the Brown Beret era. He belonged to the Bakersfield chapter and I was in the Bay Area chapter. The purpose of the Brown Berets was for the betterment of all Latinos. That old saying "The older you get, the wiser you get" had been on Cheyenne's mind; his agenda and purpose was to bring peace between the NF and the EME gangs.

Then the unthinkable happened. The story goes that one morning Cheyenne and his bodyguard, Lil' Richie from Bakersfield, were on the third tier of Palm Hall (in Chino) just talking when Richie was forced into a fight by a group of NF members. He was separated from Cheyenne and beaten to within an inch of his life. At the same time, another group of NF members attacked Cheyenne, beating and stabbing him repeatedly. They then threw his body over the third tier railing to an overhang on the second tier. The assailants then ran down the stairs and continued to beat, kick, and stab him just to make sure he was dead.

Because of the killing of Cheyenne, from that time forward there would never be peace between the NF and the EME. Cheyenne's dream died with him. The hatred and animosity between the two gangs lives on to this day.

Later Cheyenne was the subject of a movie called "American Me" which was the biography of his life story. It focused on his dream of uniting all Latinos instead of fighting one another in warfare. In the movie he persisted in his efforts, but even after going to the table three times the gangs could not come to an understanding. His dream would never come true. After the showing of the movie, some EME members took offense of how they and their gang were portrayed. Threats were made to some of the actors and others involved in the project. It seems you can't please everybody.

Chapter 11
The Trial
1973

Meanwhile, knowing I couldn't go to Chino because my trial with Bo started soon, Babo was transferred to Chino without me to start the reorganization process of the NF Constitution. There were some intelligent minds working on changing parts of the Constitution. One such part was the section that stated that any person who killed an enemy of the NF would automatically become a Captain. You can imagine the rise in body count and increase in Captain's numbers without this part being changed. It was amended to read that the General would be the only person who could officially promote anyone to the rank of Captain. After that change, some of the enemies of the NF were breathing easier.

Early one Monday morning, Bo and I were told we'd be going to court. We weren't shocked; we expected it sooner or later. A couple of San Joaquin Sheriff's Deputies drew the short straws to transport us to jail. When we arrived, we were put in jumpsuits and leg and wrist restraints. It was only a half an hour ride to the county jail, but after being locked down behind the walls for the past eight months, we looked forward to the ride. It was a real treat to get outside.

It was early spring, and sunny and warm. Fresh green leaves were sprouting on the trees and there were colorful brilliant flowers blooming on the freeway median strips along the way. Off the freeway and on to the city streets, the scenery was complimented by the beautiful women headed to unknown destinations dressed in springtime outfits. Yeah, the trip was an overdue treat.

The destination, not so much. We finally arrived in the underground garage of the courthouse jail. Once inside we were relieved of the shackles and put in the holding cell awaiting our first appearance. We were assigned attorneys and eventually housed in the county jail for the duration of the trial.

While in the holding cell I drifted into deep thought. Here I was again in another holding cell, pondering my future as I saw it. I was still a kid in mind and heart. I wanted to belong, to make my mark, to prove myself to my gang peers. I wasn't considering the much larger picture. I didn't really take to heart that there was no turning back from the path I turned onto, and I was sealing my own fate. I was delivering myself into a void where the journey ahead altered the course of not only my life but many others as well. There would be overwhelming consequences and far-reaching effects. I was binding myself to a destiny of inevitable sorrow and heartbreak. I wasn't thinking of that at the time, though. I just didn't care about anything except my loyalty to the Familia.

My attorney had told me that Mac, one of our own, had in fact testified against Bo and me during the grand jury investigation. Mac, the same guy who I hauled across the TV room floor while he was unconscious from his beating! This was how he showed his gratitude? This was how he professed his loyalty? Well, Mac, I thought, you are on your own as a traitor to the Nuestra Familia.

The news media had painted a picture of me as an NF hitman, on a mission because I had come from San Quentin at the time. I was looking at a possible seven-to-life if found guilty. That time could turn into twenty at the most. Again, I was asking myself, "What the hell was I thinking?"

When the trial began, and knowing what the DA had for ammunition against us, we knew we were fighting a losing battle from the start. We went ahead to jury trial anyway. Two weeks into the trial, the DA came to me with a deal that would reduce my charges to manslaughter. If I took it I'd only be looking at one-to-fifteen years. My pride and my loyalty to a brother NF stood in the way. I asked if Bo was offered the same deal. My attorney told me he didn't know, so I turned it down. When I saw Bo I asked him if he'd been offered the same deal, and he said he hadn't. He was upset when I told him what they had offered me. We took it to trial because the deal hadn't included us both. We would go down like family.

It took more than a month, including all the pretrial bickering back and forth of the attorneys before an actual verdict was rendered. The trial itself only took two days and the guilty verdicts were immediate. We both felt like we had been railroaded. When the judge came into court to pronounce sentence, we both refused, in defiance, to stand up. The judge proceeded to admonish us as to courtroom etiquette and asked us to stand again. We declined, as a statement that we didn't want any part of the madness, and we told the judge so. The judge determined that he was being disrespected and commenced to sentence us both to seven-to-life for the killing of Trashman.

Back at DVI, Peanut (the Captain) got himself put it in the hole for suspicion of inmate assault. Peanut was stirring up a hornet's nest by trying to continue to run the yard by himself from the hole, or 'in a shoe box' as they say. Peanut's First Lieutenant, Ninney, was also in the hole when I got back from court. Peanut's Second Lieutenant, Oso, was rounded up on the same charges as Peanut. That left my friend Larry as the next in line for the First Lieutenant in charge on the mainline. The reason for a constitution in an organization is to keep order. It's to keep guys in line, and to provide a chain of command so the members like Peanut, who was basically out of commission by being in the hole, from trying to play control freak.

Larry was very capable of taking charge as leader, but Peanut didn't like not being in control and tried to interfere with operations of the Family. He even solicited to have Larry hit to initiate a power struggle. This caused animosity between the brothers, both on the mainline and in the hole.

Both Oso and Ninney were on Peanut to let it go and stop trying to screw things up in the organization. Nobody wanted to help Peanut with his private little coup. Peanut asked me how I felt about the tension between him and Larry, testing me on where I stood. I thought to myself, 'Larry is a good friend of mine, but Peanut is the captain and head man for our immediate area.' I told Peanut that I didn't want to be in the middle of the situation and declined to be a part of it.

After Babo went to Chino, everyone knew major changes were coming down. There was a lot of tension in the ranks because nobody knew what to expect. To add to the tension, more NF members were finding their way to the hole for various reasons. Because of the increase in the numbers of NF brothers, the senior members decided to put the Lieutenants into the first cell on each tier where NFs were housed. This was done for two reasons. One was to keep an ear on staff, and two, to monitor the comings and goings on the tier.

When I got back from court my old cell had been repaired and I was moved back there. Sharky was still next door and we brought each other up-to-date on what had been going on. I was glad the trial was over and just as glad to be back at DVI.

Sharky was from Salinas and transferred from CMC (California Men's Colony) San Luis Obispo after a stabbing incident. He was part Filipino and part Mexican. He had a cool, collected demeanor. He was patient enough to take on the task of beginning to school me on the ways of the organization, which began with my abrasive attitude. He explained to me that in order to survive and make my way, I'd have to learn how to control this. I was still a wild youngster, but I guess he saw something in me, maybe potential as a future leader. Whatever it was, he took the time and accepted the challenge. Time was something we had plenty of. He taught me how to read and showed me the importance of loyalty and dedication to the organization, as well as the do's and don'ts. Sharky was a lot more experienced than I was, and I appreciated him taking the time to do all of that.

Over the months, I began to understand about controlling my anger and being able to stay in control of various situations. Sharky helped me to understand that I didn't have friends or family in the organization, only brothers. When he explained this, it helped me to understand better my personal conflict regarding the power struggle between Larry and Peanut. Things were still tense on the tier, and I knew it would be best if I didn't get involved with the Larry-Peanut situation, even though the majority were siding with Peanut.

To my surprise, one afternoon my cousin Lil' Poyo from Oakland arrived on the tier. It had been a while since I last had seen him, and it was good to see him now. He was a few cells down from me, so the kites were going back and forth between us. He was still the same old Poyo that I'd known throughout the years.

Chapter 12
Boxing Matches
1973

The guards came by one afternoon and proposed setting up boxing matches between EME and NF members every Saturday night. The way it would work was we would go to the EME tier to box one week, and the next week they would come to our tier. The guards would stand on opposite ends of the tier with three cells between, forming a ring. Whoever's tier we were on members would challenge the other gang member to box. Nobody could decline a challenge, it was unacceptable.

Saturday night boxing was approved by Peanut and Ninney, and lasted about three weekends. That's when Babo came back from Chino. When Babo saw what was going on, he lost his cool and the boxing matches came to a screeching halt. Any kind of games between two adverse factions were taboo in the Nuestra Familia.

Babo had an idea of his own. His plan was that the next time the EME came to our tier, the NF brother that was boxing would force the EME opponent against the bars so he could be stabbed. This plot was foiled when staff caught wind of it and cells were searched for weapons. In the meantime, Ninney had lost his rank and Peanut was under investigation for approving the boxing activity without first checking with anyone in the higher ranks. Babo had also picked up on the tension between Larry and Peanut, and knew about the coup against Larry.

Babo had another investigation going on without my knowledge. It was against my cousin Poyo, and was from an incident that happened years before. Babo called me aside and asked my opinion about it, and wanted to know how I felt about Poyo being targeted to be hit. I told Babo that if the situation merited that action, then I would go along with it. The incident he was referring to happened in the TV room one night in C-wing, back in the '70s at DVI. Bozo was an NF from San Jose. He and Poyo were watching TV that night when out of nowhere, an unknown black guy came in and hit Bozo on the side of the head from behind. The attack was a distraction so that an EME by the name of Duke from Hazard could start stabbing Bozo in the chest and back.

Bozo was bleeding profusely, and the surprise attack had overwhelmed him. He couldn't even mount a defense. Instead of helping him, Poyo panicked and ran off to hide, showing his cowardice. He was under the bench while his friend lay mortally wounded, breathing his last breath. When I found out the facts of why Poyo was under scrutiny, I told Babo I would go by the book if I was facing the same situation.

I asked Babo if I could make the hit myself. He reminded me that I had just been sentenced for murder, and my plate was already full. I told him I had a plan for the hit; there would be four guys on the tier in the morning when the tier tenders were out for cleaning. One of the four could be Poyo, the other three were me, Albert, and Snake. I'd make the hit while the others looked out. Again, Babo told me to stay out of it and not get involved. He said to tell Albert and Snake to make the hit instead, and for me to pass that order along.

When I told them about it, they didn't respond. When I took the knives to Albert and Snake they refused to complete the order. When I got back to Babo and told him what had transpired, he said not to worry about it. He had a backup plan. He decided to send Peanut and Oso as a sort of discipline for the boxing fiasco. They were also going to be demoted for their bad choice. I volunteered yet again to do the hit, my youthful enthusiasm and ambition rising to the surface. I knew I could do it but I wasn't looking down the road and seeing the bigger picture. I just wanted to be a part of action, and prove myself to Babo and the organization. Babo did, however, allow me to set the operation up, telling the hitters what and how it was going to go down.

Babo confided in me that two other hits were going to happen the same day around the same time. Besides Poyo, there was Fat Mike and Manny from Salinas. Fat Mike had run away from his responsibility with the hits on Bullwinkle and Diamond at Susanville. Manny would face his punishment for running away while another brother, Huero, was attacked and died from his wounds.

The next morning begin normally. It was just another day as far as everybody else was concerned. We had corn meal mush and French toast. You would never have known what was about to unfold. Babo told me that between 9:30 and 10:00 the plan would kick into action. The mainline population was released to yard and everyone went outside as usual. Fat Mike was walking laps with two other NF members, talking about nothing in particular. It was sunny and clear, about 70°, a perfect day. Fat Mike didn't know he had eaten his last breakfast.

The two NF's with Fat Mike we're leading him toward Dead Man's Alley like a lamb to slaughter. When they got near the spot they made sure no staff were in eye-shot and sort of drifted in that direction. Suddenly they pulled out their blades and pounced on Fat Mike. One blade caught him in the jugular, which caused warm blood to start pumping out in rhythm with his heartbeat. The other brother stabbed him in the upper torso. It was swift and deadly. In a matter of seconds Fat Mike was no more, bleeding out and laying in his own blood. Staff saw the two assailants fleeing the scene covered in blood. The alarm sounded and they were quickly busted.

When the alarm sounded from Fat Mike's demise, that was the signal for the hit on Lil' Manny to begin. He was forced into his cell and stabbed about forty times. The assailants stuffed him under his bunk and proceeded to wash themselves off in his sink. They changed clothes and casually left like nothing had happened. Then they drank coffee and waited for the next unlock. What they didn't expect was for Lil' Manny to somehow muster up enough strength to stagger out of his cell and manage to get onto the tier before collapsing. He did in fact survive his wounds.

When the second alarm sounded for the hit on Lil' Manny, it meant that Poyo was next. I was near the front of the tier on the punching bag keeping point. I was also acting as cover to block what was going on from the view of the staff. Poyo was hit before he knew what was happening. He got it multiple times in the chest, head, and back. At one point, he was stabbed in the eye, and liquid squirted out. Another blade sliced into his spinal cord, which caused his legs to collapse beneath him. His wounds totaled an excess of 60 holes. That was the third and final alarm. Emergency lockdown followed.

I had to walk past Poyo to get to my cell. He was laying there crying, his eyeball hanging out of its socket in a pool of blood. He was asking me to help. I just looked down at him and didn't say a word, knowing I couldn't do anything. I just shook my head and kept walking. I heard later that he survived the wounds, but lost his right eye, and walks with a cane and a limp.

The three hits that day sounded the alarm to the administration that the Nuestra Familia were cleaning their own house and putting things in order. This also alerted other prison administrations of possible similar activities. Before the dust had settled, three of our own had been hit by our own brothers, and we were on total lockdown pending investigation of the three incidents. By the afternoon, it was extremely quiet in the building and on the tier. Everybody was in shock at what had happened. I had a restless sleep that night. Poyo was my cousin after all, but he still screwed up, losing respect with the Familia. The next morning both Albert and Snake locked it up (went into protective custody) for fear of what would happen to them for refusing to hit Poyo. They knew they were in danger. That was the first protective custody move ever at DVI.

Over the next two weeks I had questions on my mind that needed resolving. I asked Babo to help me understand particularly why we, the NF, were at war with the EME. Why was Mexican fighting Mexican? I wasn't really in favor of this. From my Brown Beret days and history, I felt that warring against one another just seemed wrong and senseless. I knew if anybody could tell me it would be Babo. So he started telling me how it all started, how the EME came into existence and how the war began.

It was in the 1950s that the EME came about. They started as a prison gang. They were dealing drugs, prostituting homosexuals, gambling, and other money-making vices. They were also preying on weaker inmates. Then sometime in the '60s, one Sunday morning, five individuals were sitting around pondering on how they could make it better among the Mexican people. These guys had compassion for the Mexican inmates and didn't like the way they were being treated by the EME. There have been several little skirmishes between both sides but nothing serious. At that time the NF and the EME we're just sort of getting along, tolerating one another.

Cheyenne, a leader of the EME, saw that the two gangs were beginning to bump heads and that communications were breaking down. He was trying to keep the peace. Babo went on to tell me how the actual war broke out between the gangs. It was at San Quentin over some shoes.

An NF member named Hector (Mad Dog) from San Jose had a pair of brown Romeos. This was no ordinary pair of shoes. Hector had put a lot of work into them. Top-of-the-line Romeo's are considered prime goods, especially brown ones, and Hector was looking to sell them for canteen items. Meanwhile, there was this EME member named Mosco (Fly) who showed some interest in the shoes and asked Hector if he could check them out for a few days. What Hector didn't know was that Mosco had a reputation for ripping guys off. He was about six-foot-two, a hefty 350 pounds, and he never intended to pay Hector. After a couple of days Hector was going on a visit and jammed Mosco, telling him he either wanted the money or the shoes. Mosco informed Hector that, "It wasn't going to happen… you're burnt!"

Hector knew he had a problem at this point. He knew he would have to retaliate not only against Mosco, but against the EME for disrespecting him by stealing his shoes. The EME already had their own plans. That afternoon they drew first blood by hitting Hector, and the two other NF members on the upper yard. They then pushed their luck by hitting four other NF members on the lower yard, all at the same time. The prison was in chaos, alarms going off all over the place. Nobody was critically injured, but San Quentin was on lock down for investigation into the incidents. They later decided to remove all the NF from Quentin and basically gave it over to the EME. When Babo became General he declared war on them and stated that there would never be peace because of those vicious attacks on the NF that day. And that's how the war started over a pair of shoes.

Meanwhile I continued my schooling from some of the older guys like Ninney, Shark, and Peanut. I was anxious and motivated to learn all I could. I also knew the more I learned, the more responsibility I would inherit. I was getting in deep, but it was what I lived for.

The NF was pretty much dominating the hole. More and more members were showing up there, especially after the hits. Because there were so many of us, there was a need to spread the leaders out throughout the building in order to control things the most efficient way. There were other changes going on in the NF at the same time. Babo promoted Larry to Captain to pick up where Peanut left off. Larry had held his position even while dealing with adversity from Peanut, so it was a good promotion. Peanut would never again hold rank in the Familia. He lacked leadership skills and had sunk his own boat.

Another change made was to promote me to Lieutenant, my first rank ever. It was an unpopular choice for many other members. There was a little animosity because some of the guys didn't know me that well. Some were jealous and thought Babo was showing me favoritism. As seventh Lieutenant, I was assigned to the first tier and in charge of punishment and/or initiation. I think I was promoted because of my eagerness to learn about the organization and its inner workings.

Babo saw in me what others didn't. He saw my potential as a leader, and nobody questioned his actions. He saw that I was ready to move up in ranks and leave the nest. He thought I was ready to take the responsibility of commanding soldiers on my own, to have guys under me. That meant I would have to be relocated to another tier without divulging the reasons to staff. I didn't really want to move. I had made friends and some of those guys helped me get to where I was.

Babo believed in me. He knew I could do it, and I wasn't going to let him down. Some of the members knew what was going on, and knew I took my job seriously. They weren't sure whether they should fear me or appreciate and trust me. Only time would tell, and they would get their answers.

Chapter 13
Lieutenant
1973

Soon after that I moved to my new surroundings, and began my new assignment as Lieutenant on the lowest tier. There literally was no sunshine. It was dark with no lights at all. It was dingy with the stale odor of cigarette smoke, unwashed clothes, and sweaty bodies. As time went on, I was becoming accepted by the ten NF members on the tier. I was trying to make other friends without letting on that I was still a little wet behind the ears as a leader. I had an outgoing personality which put others at ease. This would change because of some things happening that brought dark clouds of negativity to dampen my spirits.

First, Babo had been transferred to Soledad where Death Row Joe was housed. This happened because administration wanted to keep those two NF leaders together. I lost a good friend and mentor when that went down. The BGF hit a guard and killed him. This resulted in another prolonged lockdown investigation, which meant anyone standing in or near the vicinity of the incident, BGF, NF, EME, it didn't matter, were rounded up and sent to the hole pending investigation.

With the hole becoming more crowded with the influx of suspects from the latest incident, staff were making wholesale moves. That meant putting enemies of the NF on the tier. It wasn't a good idea and made a bad situation worse by tossing enemies into the mix.

One thing did occur that happened to lift my spirits a bit was that my old friend Flapper showed up and was assigned to my cell during the roundup of suspects. Staff were doubling us up, tossing in an extra mattress to accommodate the increased population in the hole. Flapper was also glad to see me. We brought each other up-to-date from when we'd seen each other last, two years before. Flapper was very informative, and a big help to me in adjusting to my new position.

Flapper was a hell of a guy. He didn't talk much, and when he did he was very low-key and soft-spoken, never showing any emotion. He was also very experienced and loyal to the NF. I had never been a religious person, but when Flapper's familiar face showed up that day, I knew somebody up there was looking out for me. He was a big help in lowering my anxiety level.

Going back to the BGF, they were active revolutionaries fighting repression forced upon them by administration and society. I didn't know too much about them except what I'd heard from their leader George Jackson, who I knew at Soledad. He was pretty much considered a legend. Everyone knew the BGF were sworn enemies of the Aryan Brotherhood, whose organization started back at Alcatraz prison in the 1940s. They used to be called the Blue Birds. Maybe that's why they changed their name.

The BGF were allies with the NF, basically because they ran their organization a lot like we did, with ranks and chains of command. They got a lot of their training from a book called the 'Red Bible,' which included the revolutionary history of China and how they commanded armies. Other books on Castro and Cuba were popular with them. Books about Marxism and communism, that kind of stuff. The current leader of the BGF was a guy named Mudd. He was a no-nonsense kind of guy. When he spoke, he commanded undivided attention. I would get to know him very well.

I was still conflicted about why the NF and EME had to keep their war going. It seemed counterproductive. We were all Mexicans. You had to fight with guys you used to be friends with or went to school with, or went to church with. Mudd told me that sometimes wars are fought over the most trivial matters or misunderstandings… sometimes merely over an insult. "War was war" he would say.

My position as Lieutenant was about to be put to the test. Word came down that a homosexual named Tina, who lived on my tier, was to be hit in retaliation for setting up an NF member for a hit. I'd had a lot of other tasks that had been handled with no problem, but this one was going to have to be done through the bars, and that was something new to me. Not being too experienced with this kind of operation I sent the kite out to NF members looking for a volunteer.

I thought I'd have guys lining up for this one, but the response was so quiet that you could have heard a tier mouse pushing a cotton ball. Not one person volunteered. I told Flapper about the situation, and I told him I planned to just do it myself. Problem solved. He reminded me that because of my rank as a Lieutenant, I don't make hits. That's what soldiers are for. Then he said he'd do it. This wasn't the first time Flapper had spoken up and wanted to do a hit. What I didn't know was that he was dying of cirrhosis of the liver. (Flapper died of that illness in 1978.)

We started formulating a plan to hit Tina the next morning. The day started out as usual; breakfast and a minor cleanup while waiting for the exercise period to open on the tier. At about 8:30 AM Tina came out and was walking around, not a care in the world. I called him to my cell and he approached with caution, wondering why I would be calling. I joked around and eased his mood, like a spider to a fly enticing him into the web. He let his guard down and approached. That's when Flapper came up and with lightning speed speared him in the side.

Tina's eyes opened to the size of golf balls. He turned and ran, screaming, "I've been hit!" I threw water to wash off the cell walls and tried to clean the tier before staff arrived. Flapper broke the knife and flushed it down the toilet. Staff arrived and cuffed up Flapper and me as they searched our cells for evidence. The only thing they found was some diluted blood mostly washed away by water. We were on lockdown for two days while they investigated. Tina never said who hit him or why. He was relocated to another tier in the hole with the group rejects calling themselves the 'Brown Bear Party.' Another wannabe gang.

After we were released from lockdown, Mudd called me over to have a talk with me. He proceeded to school me about being a Lieutenant in charge. He said that when an assignment is to be accomplished, you don't ask for volunteers. You command your soldiers to carry out your orders. He went on to say that joking and playing around with soldiers is forbidden. It shows weakness in those in command. He also told me I should be more serious with soldiers for their own good and protection. From that day on I embraced change to keep my soldiers more focused. My mission was to keep them alive, as long as they followed orders.

A month after the investigation, no charges were filed for the hit on Tina, and Flapper was paroled. I was left to myself and thought about what he and Mudd had told me. I sent a kite down the tier to inform everyone that from now on, nobody was to play games or joke around with me. If anyone needed to talk with me, it had to be about family business and family business only.

Six months later, myself, as well as the rest of the tier, seemed to have adjusted pretty well to the changes I'd initiated. The investigation into the hit on that guard had concluded, and with that the population in the hole had been reduced. It was time for more changes. My time in rank and increasing experience led to an advancement, I was now Third Lieutenant. With the promotion came more responsibility. That also meant relocation.

Before being relieved, I had to recommend someone to take my place on the tier I was leaving. I didn't have the power to appoint, but I could suggest. I chose Slow Ed, an older, more experienced brother that came from Soledad North due to an adverse transfer. I felt confident in my suggestion, and the final stamp of approval came down from the Captain, which was Larry. Larry was doing really well in his position. He kept the organization running smoothly.

I was ordered to move to the second tier on the opposite side of the building to reorganize the NF on that tier. I was basically starting a new regiment. I went into the first cell on the second tier, as all NF Lieutenants did. Sharky came with me, he was a valued asset, especially after Flapper's parole.

The Nuestra Familia had key people in every job position throughout the prison. There were cooks, R&R workers, laundry, canteen, and hallway porters. Porters were basically NF escorts to provide protection from other gangs, even though prison guards were always around, no chances were taken. All the watches had NF eyes and ears, all the time. There were several NF members on the tier; Red Bone from Riverside County, Sharky, and Charlie, all known as the CMC boys. Lil' T-bone from San Jose took care of business when needed. It was coming together.

Chapter 14
The Grief

The reception I received when I first came to the second tier was a little bit chilly. Word had gotten around that I ran a tight ship. This was for their own protection. They would soon appreciate why I was like this. It wasn't a popularity contest. I took my rank and job seriously and everybody knew that. NF training on the Constitution went on daily, along with other training in knife-making, zip guns, hand-to-hand combat, anatomy, and other warfare curriculum. I made sure the NF members used their time wisely.

It was all going well until I received word that Apache on the third tier had to be hit. He had supposedly set up two NF members at Soledad Central. The guys that had been hit were Crackers, a friend of mine, and another guy named Chief. Apache had been hit once already and was in the hole as a result. He sent word down to me that he wanted to talk. So, we set up a time to communicate through the tele-commode. What he told me was that he didn't set anybody up, and he wanted to move down to my tier. This kind of set me aback. He was being forthright and seemed sincere. I put him off for the time being. This put me in an awkward position. I sent word to the mainline that I'd talked with Apache, and I believed him when he said he hadn't done what he was accused of. Word came back to stay out of it and just make the hit.

Apache was adamant in his insistence that he was innocent, and asked again to move to my tier. I went ahead with the move, figuring I could talk with him face-to-face and maybe clear this thing up. He was moved the following day and we talked. Afterwards, I was convinced he was telling the truth and I sent word that I thought we ought to at least verify his story. The answer came back, "Make the hit!"

I was really going out on a limb for Apache because I didn't believe he did what he was accused of. I sent another kite, this one to Larry, the Captain, and my friend. I asked him to check on this. I told him I had moved Apache to my tier and anybody who was guilty would not have made that move unless he was really stupid or very sly. A day or so later, Larry sent this message back to me:

> Joey,
>
> We've been friends a long time. I understand you are having a problem with a decision that has already been made. I did check on your request to verify this matter. He sounds convincing, but that's his nature when in trouble. THE HIT STILL STANDS! Any further questions about this action will make me very uncomfortable about my decision with your future. Continue your firm action as the leader that I know you are.
>
> Larry

With that very much to-the-point warning from Larry, I had no other choice. The hit had to be made. Next, I had to choose two NF members to do the work. I didn't know it at that the time, but I would soon discover at the ripe old age of twenty years the facts of life pertaining to grief. I reluctantly chose Charlie and Sharky, due to their experience, to carry out the order. I had them come by and pick up the knives during exercise time, and instructed them to make the hit the next morning when Apache was playing chess at the far end of the tier. That night I couldn't sleep. I knew in my heart this was not right. My restlessness was caused by turmoil in my conscience with what I knew was wrong. But my own survival depended on following orders without question. It was a very long night.

After breakfast the next morning I just sat in my cell sticking my little mirror out the bars so I could see down to the end of the tier. It was business as usual. Everybody was doing something to pass the time. Then the sounds of scuffling, screams of pain, and fighting erupted. Apache was putting up a good fight. He worked out regularly and it showed, but he was still recovering from the first hit. T-bone broke the knives and flushed them down the toilet. The guards heard the chaos and ran down the catwalk, sounding the alarm. Everybody was ordered to lock it up. Apache managed to walk up the tier towards the bar gate, right next to my cell. He looked me in the eyes and asked, "Why? I told you the truth, Joey. Why didn't you believe me? I did not do what was said. I thought you were my friend."

Believe me, I have felt bad before but now I felt worse as I listened to what Apache said, and watched him standing there dripping blood. This wasn't easy for me either. I just told him, "Go on to the dispensary and get patched up." I watched him turn away and walk off in pain, never looking back. I was overwhelmed in my own heart because I knew he was telling the truth. Apache survived his wounds, his second hit in a month. He was transferred out of DVI.

The tier was on lockdown for two days for investigation. Charlie and Sharky were rolled up and sent to the bottom tier in enemy territory with the Brown Bear party. The BBs were trying to make allies with the EMEs.

The bottom tier was divided into three sections. Charlie was housed in the first section near the gate, and Sharky was housed in the rear. After a few days, Sharky met a wannabe gang member name Lil' Puppet. What he didn't know was that Lil' Puppet wanted to be in the EME. It was his dream. For this to happen he would have to hit an NF member to be accepted, and that member unfortunately was Sharky.

Less than a week later I was schooling NF members on tactics when my heart was grieved again. I received the news of Sharky's death. Lil' Puppet had stabbed him in the heart through the bars. It happened while he offered Sharky a cigarette, completely catching him by surprise. When Sharky realized what had happened, it was too late. When staff told Puppet to lock it up so they could get Sharky out to medical, Puppet refused until he knew Sharky was dead. Staff couldn't enter the tier to render aid until it was safe to do so. By the time they reached Sharky, he was gone. This was one of my worst months ever. I went into deep mourning. We went on lockdown for the investigation. I kept asking myself how the hell this had happened. I felt Sharky had been set up and I wanted answers.

The administration knew that this could erupt into a very explosive problem. They also knew my reputation and were afraid of what I might do in retaliation. I was called to the program office to speak with the P.A. and the Captain. They were correct in their concern; I was pissed. Mainly because I felt it was my fault that Sharky had been put in that position. But I also wanted to know why Sharky was housed with the Brown Bear Party, known sympathizers to the EME. He should have been put in a cell up front near Charlie. They didn't have any answers for that. They explained to me how Lil' Puppet got to Sharky and it only fed the fire that was burning inside me. I told them that someone was going to pay dearly for what had happened, and that I wanted Charlie moved to the second tier for his protection since they couldn't do the job. I was upset and leading with my emotions. The whole institution was put on lockdown status. No yard. No program. No nothing. During feeding time staff were taking no chances. They were using fiberglass shields for protection when handing us trays through the tray slots.

After four days, it was still quiet. Nothing happening on the tiers or in the entire prison. Nothing was going to happen until I talked with the administration again. I got word from my Captain to go talk to them again so we could get off lockdown. This had been a cooling off time for me, and a time for grieving. My hatred had begun to subside and I was regaining my composure. The whole time we were on lockdown nobody complained to me. Now it was time for me to think about what was best for the organization, to do what I was told, and get the program going. I sent word to the prison administration to set up a meeting.

The meeting began with small talk and condolences about what happened to Sharky. I apologized for my outburst of rage at the peak of the chaos, and they told me they understood. I again requested that

Charlie be moved back to the second tier. The talks went well and seemed productive, because within hours afterward full program was restored. It was welcome news to the whole population. From that point forward, the respect I was getting from staff and convicts alike was noticeable. I felt an internal aura of power, like a king ruling over his people.

Charlie didn't get moved back to the second tier. As a matter of fact, he disappeared altogether. Word was he was transferred to an undisclosed prison, however, he was alive. I think Charlie felt that something might happen to him because of what happened to Sharky. In the meantime, Lil' Puppet wasn't making any points with the District Attorney. During the trial for Sharky's murder, he somehow acquired a knife and attacked the prosecuting ADA, wounding him. At sentencing, not only did he get seven-to-life for killing Sharky, but another nine-to-life for his attempted murder of the prosecuting attorney. That pretty much sealed his fate.

Speaking of fate and karma, Lil' Puppet's dreams of becoming a bonafide EME gang member were dashed when he celled up with the brother of an EME member who got tired of his boasting about killing Sharky. He was using Sharky as a trophy in his attempts to become an EME. The EME cellmate stabbed Puppet to shut him up. Satisfaction flooded my mind when I learned of this, but he lived to see another day. I ran into him years later. He looked old. He stabbed a guy in Folsom and was sent to Pelican Bay State Prison, never to be seen or heard from again.

Chapter 15
MCU Program

A program was initiated in the in the hole, East Hall at DVI, called Management Control Unit Program (MCU). This program was started as an incentive for those who remained disciplinary free, having no write-ups for one year. We were selected to participate in the program before entering back to the mainline yard. There were approximately 300 convicts participating in this unit. Each inmate had his own room or space, a larger exercise yard, and could go to a chow hall for meals. This was a big improvement from what we had. We were earning our way back to the mainline.

Eventually the administration made other positive changes in the system. One change designed to keep the peace between the rival gangs was housing them at separate facilities throughout the state. All of DVI at Tracy was for Nuestra Familia. Soledad Central was for dropouts and gang members who no longer wanted to be involved with violence. San Quentin and Folsom was dedicated to the EME and ABs. CMC and Vacaville were considered neutral ground for all gangs. No exceptions. This was working, peace was happening.

Time passed, and before I knew it I'd gone several years clean with no major problems or disciplinary write-ups. Several times I had to help the administration to keep minor problems from escalating into full-blown brawls. Stabbings were at an all-time low. There were some things between individuals that were beyond my control, but I had kept the peace for the most part. After going to annual committee meetings over the years, and having been rejected in attempts to go back to the mainline, I stopped going. I was tired of going in there and being asked what I had done to improve myself. There was nothing to look forward to. The results were always the same, I was rejected.

One afternoon prior to another annual review, the CC–II (Counselor), Mr. Kane, called me in for a pre-committee meeting. I told him I didn't want anything to do with it. I reminded him of all the other times. I didn't want to get false hopes going. This time, however, he told me I should attend. He told me I might have a surprise in store.

Two days later I went before committee. As I stepped in the room I saw the facility Captain, the Program Administrator, and Mr Kane. They were all seated behind a large table going over paperwork. After introductions, which were for the record and not really necessary, Mr. Kane read an overview of why I was in the hole, and what I'd been doing for myself during this time. Then he went on to say some good things about me. That was a surprise. It was the first time I was ever given positive remarks about anything I had done. At the end of the hearing I was approved for the MCU program at East Hall, which I'd been hearing so much about. I was speechless and when the committee asked me if I had anything to say, all I could manage was a sincere thank you and a brief acknowledgment that I appreciated the chance to attend this program. I left with a smile on my face.

Later on I was surprised to find out that Babo, DR, Mousey from San Jose, and Crow from Salinas were at MCU also. They were transferred from Soledad Central, along with Dicky Bird, who didn't fit the criteria for MCU and ended up on the mainline.

It usually took Sacramento thirty days to approve any committee action regarding MCU program transfers to East Hall. I was upset when I heard a couple of guards talking about some company donating black and white TVs that were going to cells in the hole. Here it was 1975, and after doing all those years without a TV or anything, now they were finally allowing them and I was leaving. Just my luck. The electricians were installing the wiring and outlets for not only TVs but lights as well. That would be a big improvement after all those years in the dark.

When the electricians came to our tier we all had to be temporarily moved for the job to be done. At that time I was moved to East Hall.

But prior to my leaving I had to find a replacement. I settled on an NF member named Apple from New York. He was a Puerto Rican who hadn't liked the accommodations in San Quentin and had tried to escape in the '60s.

After that he had been transferred to Soledad. He'd come down with Babo, DR, and the rest of them. They had all been schooled by Babo and DR, so they all got rank before the NF members at DVI. I had been watching Apple and noticing how he carried himself with the other members. He was bright and patient and took his responsibilities seriously. He was my recommendation for my replacement. Larry never doubted or questioned my decisions or choices and endorsed Apple for the position. That was the good news. Now for the bad news. Whenever any Lieutenant in charge is moved or transferred to another yard or institution, he loses rank and goes back to the rank of soldier until seen fit for promotion back to Lieutenant.

I fully expected this to be the case with me. It was what was taught to us in our schooling. I gave Apple the rundown on all his soldiers so he'd have a better understanding of individual capabilities and what he was dealing with. I knew I'd chosen the right man for the job.

It was barely two months after Dicky Bird hit the mainline when he ended up in the hole. He had been at CMC and was with a gang called Familia Cinco (Family Five) before coming to DVI. The FC was a gang who attempted to get started at CMC, but never got off the ground because their members went into the NF or the EME. He was told that he would have to make a hit. An AB had got out to the line somehow and was in the kitchen one day. Dicky Bird saw him and took off on him, stabbing him as best he could. The AB was fighting back, and by luck, knocked the knife out of Dicky Bird's hand. By chance, Smiley from Salinas was there and ran over to help Dicky Bird. Dicky Bird, Smiley, and Bones, who happened to be in the area, were all rolled up for investigation.

Meanwhile, Babo had been released from East Hall back to the mainline. After getting settled, he sought out Larry to start working on strengthening up the organization. When I arrived at East hall, the

Lieutenant in charge was Mousey from San Jose. Mousey was a character. He was an ugly old coot, too. With his scruffy beard, he looked like a troll trying to find his bridge. There was no question as to how he had been given that nickname.

I noticed everyone, including the tier leader, was NF. That was a relief. There was another Lieutenant named 'Sapo' (Frog) there who was not very popular with a few of us. Sapo was one of the members who hit Fat Mike at Dead Man's Alley. He was charged but never convicted of the hit on Fat Mike. Something about Sapo didn't sit right with me. It was just a feeling I had.

I was assigned my own room with lights. What a concept! I also found out we could have our own black and white TV, so I asked a family member to send one in. Even though it was only a black and white, this was a huge improvement. A guy could get comfortable with all these perks. One of the tier tenders told me DR wanted to talk with me later. The next day I headed to the yard.

I saw a lot of faces I knew. Some I'd worked for, others had been under my command. There was a new gang called Bad Company, an offshoot of the AB, and white guys who were NF sympathizers. Another gang out of San Francisco, the 'Jose Fong Boys', were also NF sympathizers. They had a colorful past from the 70's when they massacred an adversary group meeting at San Francisco's Golden Dragon restaurant. Joe Fong's brother died. They'd received a lot of notoriety when they bloodied these guys up.

I noticed DR heading my way. We embraced and were glad to see one another. We chatted briefly before getting down to business. We established schedules for schooling the soldiers, and went over plans to strengthen and improve the unity within the Nuestra Familia.

After moving to East Hall I didn't stay a soldier for long. Mousey was in the home stretch of doing his time. DR knew my reputation as a leader and chose me to fill Mousey's position when he went home. My training started all over again and I spent most of my time at Mousey's side. A general meeting of all the tier Lieutenants was held. DR informed the other members that I would be taking over for Mousey as First Lieutenant and deserved the same respect they would give Mousey. The NF came out with a new Constitution for the streets, and Mousey would be schooling the soldiers that were getting out within ninety days. The new constitution was called The Sub-Division.

As for me taking over, there were some hoots and boos when DR delivered the message to the gang. There were a few members who weren't sure about me, and some didn't like the fact that there was a new sheriff in town. That meant changes would be made. One of those changes was that I informed Sapo that he was going to be demoted. It wasn't because of what he did to Fat Mike. He was just one of those guys that you knew in your heart wasn't any good. Sapo was mad at me for this, and told me he was going to complain to Larry. When I took command, Sapo was demoted. Larry talked with me about the move. I told him it wasn't personal. It was due to Sapo's lack of experience as a leader. Later, Sapo went into the federal witness protection program. Like I said, sometimes you just have a feeling about a guy.

Every Lieutenant has a tier commander (TC) who is equal to a Sergeant. A TC takes temporary command when the Lieutenant isn't available. As such, the TC is basically the right-hand man to the Lieutenant of each tier. My TC was called up ninety percent of the time when I was off the tier for meetings, or whatever came up. When Mousey went home I would have approximately two hundred soldiers under my command. DR was schooling me on tactics and other meaningful operations. It was a good thing he did, because two weeks later Mousey paroled and DR was transferred to the mainline.

Throughout my years as a Lieutenant my formal training as a leader continued, and I acquired lots of experience and responsibility. I had to make decisions every day. Some were easy, some not so easy. Decisions were made to benefit the Family. One day I received word, or should I say received an order, that required all my years of experience and my own personal judgement to deal with. I was shocked when I got that command. I know what the Constitution said and I know what the rules are. I was to obey all orders as directed from the top. For God's sake, though, it seemed no one was safe in this game. The order was to hit Peanut!

Here was a member who had always been a loyal, devoted member to the NF. I couldn't believe my ears. A hit on Peanut. The same Peanut who had taken me under his wing to help make me what I was today. He was a friend and I wanted to know "why". What could he have done so wrong to deserve to be hit? It turned out he had disobeyed a couple of orders given to him regarding some petty things that happened sometime ago in another regiment. I went to bat for him and spoke up.

I ran my objections along to Larry, and reminded him all the things Peanut had done to get the NF to where it was today. I told him how Peanut had schooled me and others to make the NF run more efficiently. Larry did take this into consideration, and thought about the request to reconsider Peanut's punishment. He had to be dealt with in some way or the other, though. Larry informed me that he decided he would turn Peanut over to me and to make him my responsibility. He told me to handle him in any way I saw fit and that he knew I would make it right.

Later I talked with Peanut about the orders to have him hit. He was really shaken up by this news. I guess I would be shaking too if I had just been told I had a hit out on me. I told him that whatever it was that he had done in another regiment in the past, it was over. Whatever it was he did or didn't do, from this day was ancient history. Peanut was greatly relieved and thankful for what I did for him.

Chapter 16
The Nuestra Familia Bank

All First Lieutenants were in place in their respective positions. I oversaw the East Hall and kept things running smoothly. The NF pretty much dominated DVI in every aspect of everyday program, from having key people in certain jobs to where the NF was aware of any 'unwanted guests' that entered their domain, or who left a tier, yard, or even the prison. This was a really elaborate system and the NF had perfected it over time.

As we expanded, new projects were coming together to fund and support the broadening family network. First, we set up a bank to receive incoming revenue. This was known as the Regimental Bank. Money was raised by various means, such as running a personal store operated by an NF member, and selling donated items. Then the NF started selling drugs that came in from the streets. There was gambling revenue from card games, dice, betting on sports, horse racing, poker tables. Gambling happened on the mainline and in each wing. Another money-making venture was prostitution. After being inside for so many years away from females, some guys give in and turn towards their own kind for satisfaction. It happens still, and all the proceeds end up in the Regimental Bank of the Nuestra Familia.

Soon after, some of the proceeds went into buying TVs for NF members. Other money was reinvested in drugs or supplies needed to keep the incoming flow going. Yes, everything was coming together. The administration was aware of all this going on and turned a blind eye. They didn't want to know the details so long as peace was kept.

Communication among the highest ranks between Babo, Larry, and with DR on the mainline was well established. We had our bases covered and contingency plans for whatever situations might come up. What we didn't expect was that a contingency plan would have to kick in within nine months. Larry informed us that he was to go home on parole.

We had plenty of time for contingency plans in this case to find a suitable reserve to take Larry's place. The eligible candidates for the job were: Dicky Bird, Apple, or myself. One of us would be the new Captain, and the decision was a task in itself.

It was a warm sunny June Saturday morning. The yard had just been released when I was given an envelope by Larry with a copy of the Sub-Division to the Constitution for the streets in it. Members were required to participate in an NF pre-release schooling program to show them the ways and means of the Sub-Division, and how to connect with the Lieutenants in their regiments on the street. We had to keep all members in the loop for future endeavors in business ventures and training. With Larry going home soon, steps were being taken toward organizing crime to support the NF, on the streets and inside as well. There were already other NF members who were doing things to bring in money for the family.

Jesse James from Stockton was organizing the drug cartel for his neighborhood, also known as a regiment. He had pretty much corralled the business end of card clubs and entertainment clubs by selling them protection services.

Mousy paroled to San Jose, and had been organizing hit squads to take out NF dropouts that were getting in the way of conducting business, which was on the increase. Things were starting to move in the direction that the Sub-Division was set up for.

Casper in Salinas was being schooled by Art Bee, who had a pool hall and some hotels on tap. They were also working with drug sales. Bun-Head Huerto of Hayward had a regiment in the making, but was having a difficult time. The EME was already established there and were trying to get stronger. Competition between members ignited in varying degrees, but Bun Head was contributing. He was executed in Salinas sometime later. Crackers had a company in his regiment with Sammy Vee from Fresno. Crackers had no leadership skills and was having problems, so word was sent for Sammy Vee to take over in Fresno. Crackers was not happy about that. An internal war between him and Sammy broke out. Crackers ended up leaving the NF in disgrace and started his own group called F-14's. Years later they became the Fresno Bulldogs.

Watsonville had their own regiment with an NF member named Cat. I don't know how he got that nickname, but I would have liked to know. As more and more parolees were released from prison and found their way onto the streets, crime rates begin to rise. Authorities on both sides of the prison walls noticed these facts and were in search of solutions to control the crime spree.

Chapter 17
Special Security Unit

Thus was born the Special Security Unit (SSU). It was a powerful unit of specially trained men, all of whom were Lieutenants with the California Department of Corrections. Some were also parole agents with years of experience under their belts and had training regarding prison gangs. The SSU had as much power as a mini FBI unit, in that they had the same access to information. The SSU were trained in watching gangs and their activities, and had a working understanding of each group and its members.

That's where the females of the gangs came into use. They were being used as mules to traffic drugs, move information, product and cash, right in plain sight under the noses of the SSU who were concentrating their focus on the male members of these gangs. Linda was a girl that liked the gang life. She was with Cat first, then went with Babo. She was like a silent partner, helping Babo with the behind-the-scenes jobs. She was very wise in her ways and kept the other girls in check. Brown Eyes, Forty-Four, and Mayann were just a few of the girls loyal to the NF and their cause, and could be counted on no matter what they were asked to do.

Those women were an asset to the NF in times of need, and went to the next level of dedication to confirm this fact.

Chapter 18
Blind Spot

Communication between allies is a necessity when working closely together. For example, when a hit is about to happen within another gang or group, depending if it's NF or BGF, the leaders of the group doing the hit will notify the leaders of their allies so that no conflict or misunderstanding occurs between the groups. With that said, I had a real good friend who I had known for about a year. His name was Paul and he was an African-American. We shared the weight pile together and talked about mutual interests. Paul was involved with the Crips, a gang from Los Angeles known for violence. He'd given up the violence of that past lifestyle to better himself. He'd been approached and asked to join the BGF, and politely refused.

Whenever I was out on the weight pile I always had two or three bodyguards with me, and not the Department of Corrections type. It's insurance, you see. My position as First Lieutenant did have its perks, and one was protection 24/7, especially on the weight pile. That area is located within a blind spot where staff can't see what's going on. There's a lot of guys milling around, and the equipment gets in the way. They just don't have a clear eye-line of everything. Things can happen to a guy… bad things.

One sunny afternoon Paul was working out on the pile behind me. I was working out up front and talking with him and some other guys. Mostly we were hitting the iron, and huffing and puffing away. One of my Lieutenants came up and whispered in my ear that we had to leave the pile, "Right now!" The BGF had notified him that a hit was about to go down and for us to get clear of the area. When I asked who the target was my heart skipped four beats. It was Paul.! I looked in his direction but he was continuing his reps, not knowing what was about to happen to him. The reason for the hit? Just because he wanted to do the right thing and not join another gang, do his own time, go home a better human being and be with his family.

Once again, I was grieving. Paul didn't deserve this. It was a stupid sacrifice just because he didn't want to join a gang. Paul had found his ultimate life with God. I didn't want this to happened to him. I wanted to warn him of his impending doom, but my bodyguards were already on all sides and walking me away from that area. Interference was not an option anyway, because this was a BGF hit and nothing could be done. Paul didn't notice that the entire area had cleared out. He was enjoying his workout and had 250 pounds extended over his chest. He never saw the 50-pound dumbbell coming at his head. The BGF caved in his forehead, and the iron he had extended finished the job when the bar came down on his windpipe, cutting off his air. Death was immediate. My heart goes out to his family.

It took the guards twenty minutes to notice him lying there with blood dripping from his head. The alarm sounded and they finally came for him. We were on lockdown for two days for the investigation. Two weeks later, the BGF leader, Romeo, and myself, were called to the administration office. We were informed that the MCU program was being shut down because they needed East Hall. They were going to convert it to a protective custody unit. The P.A. told us that within three weeks we all would be moved to L-wing, because it was smaller in size compared to East Hall. A few lucky ones would be released back to the mainline yard.

The Captain and the P.A. suggested having Romeo and I, as the leaders of the two main gangs on the yard, inspect L-wing before moving in. The wing had two floors. The first tier had a wall divider in the middle to keep the noise level down. The second tier didn't have a wall and was open, with more room to move about. The wing even had its own kitchen, which was a plus, and the yard was about half the size of the East Hall yard. If we went along with the move, it would help to cut down on the population for those of us moving to L-wing. When we returned to East Hall I talked to the regiment, and notified Larry to bring him up to speed. Larry told me to go along with the program.

After two and a half weeks we started moving to L–wing, while selected others went to the mainline. When I moved, I made sure my right-hand man and Second Lieutenant, Casper, came with me. I trusted him with my life. He had been there for me when I needed him in the past, like on the weight pile during Paul's hit. I counted on him to be there in the future. After the move was completed I had to start all over again setting up Lieutenants for each tier, and communications. Just on those two tiers I had a total of six Lieutenants in my own regiment.

Later I got word that Larry had paroled and gone home. We had said our goodbyes a couple of weeks earlier through the internal communications system. I had been in the hole for seven years and wondered if my day would ever come. When you're doing time, any good news is a blessing. But most of the time it's just about doing the time and not letting it do you. Then, one morning I came in from the yard and was just getting ready to get some lunch when one of my bodyguards said I was being called to the counselor's office. I was thinking, "What did I do now?" With three bodyguards in tow, I was escorted to see the counselor. I hated to have bodyguards all the time, but that's the price you pay when you're in a leadership position. The NF takes good care of their own no matter how I felt about it. Someday I would be thankful those bodyguards were there for me.

After arriving at the door of the counselor's office, two of the bodyguards took off, and the last one posted up until I was finished. I knocked and was invited in. I noticed that my file was open and spread out on the desk. I waited for Mr. Kane to start talking, and when he did I couldn't believe my ears. He asked me how I felt about going back to the mainline, and if I wanted to go. It was like the whole room lit up. I stammered for words. Finally I caught my breath and a big smile appeared on my face. "When do I pack?" I replied. I couldn't believe it. Excitement didn't begin to express my elation after all those years in the hole. I felt like a kid waiting for Christmas morning.

Mr. Kane said that he was recommending me for approval to be moved to mainline at my next annual committee meeting. When committee concluded, I had been approved, and I notified DR immediately of my status change.

The next thing to do was to find my replacement. I had Casper in mind for this position, and he was basically a shoe-in to take my place. I taught him everything I knew, and had enough confidence in him that I'd already forwarded my recommendation to DR for approval. But things rarely go as planned, I would learn. Apple arrived in L–wing, and everything changed. The problem was that Apple had experience as a First Lieutenant, and he was close with DR, Mousey, Babo, and a few others who were high in the ranks. Those guys came up at Soledad and had a bond. Me and others in the ranks had been 'born' at DVI.

Word came down from DR he had chosen Apple to take my place. We all had our choice picks for replacements, and you can believe that I wasn't happy with DR's decision, but it had been made. I called Casper in to tell him the news and he wasn't happy. I reassured him that when the opportunity presented itself, he'd be my first choice to call upon. Even though he was disappointed, he understood how things worked.

I wasn't a fan of Apple after that, even though I knew he was capable of commanding the position. Because of his arrogant attitude, and the way he carried himself, I stayed away from him as much as possible. Apple was just Apple. Twenty-four hours later I found myself on the mainline in E–wing. And again, when I moved I lost my ranking and was automatically reduced to a soldier. That wouldn't last for long.

Chapter 19
DVI - Mainline
1977

Once on the yard I ran into Snake from Oakland and Randy from Fresno. DR, Dicky Bird, and Babo were all housed in H-wing. We all greeted and embraced. After the warm greeting, I was brought up to speed on the goings-on on the yard. Dicky Bird was First Lieutenant on the mainline. After being in the hole for eight years, finally going back to the mainline was a culture shock for me. It took some time to get used to it. It's like going to a stadium football game, all those people swarming around you, a little unsettling. I would get used to it, though. I was a little nervous and very much on guard. DR was walking around the yard and visiting with guys. He was escorted by bodyguards at all times. Randy was the Lieutenant in charge in E-wing at the time I arrived in L-wing. Soon thereafter DR informed me that I was replacing Randy as the Lieutenant of E-wing due to my experience. Luckily, Randy was actually relieved to hear the news. He revealed that he felt uncomfortable in the job. He was a quiet guy and kept to mostly to himself. So there was no animosity between us when I took over. I was a little upset, though. I guess I was hoping for a little vacation for a time to get used to my surroundings. Here I was taking on this full responsibility so soon after getting out of the hole. So be it.

I fell into a Second Lieutenant's rank. I was equal to Dicky Bird's rank. After two weeks taking over E-wing as a Lieutenant, I had twenty-five members under my command. I kept Randy around to give me the rundown on who had knives hidden away, and to provide instructions to everyone in E-wing. He also took me on a tour of all the blind spots, filled me in on how often the staff made rounds, and any other pertinent information that could be of value.

I was informed of a prospective new member named Philip. He was a Mexican from Los Angeles and an NF sympathizer who wanted to be in the gang. He had been in prison for a few years and had a track record that was being investigated before being admitted as a member. I didn't give it much thought at that time. Most of the potential recruits are carefully scrutinized before being allowed in, and most of them pass inspection. But occasionally, there's that one individual that's rejected. Then they're handed over to the rejection committee for final disposition, which is messy. That's where I came in.

Unfortunately, Philip failed the investigation process. It came to light that he had set up NF members in the past, and this was discovered and confirmed. Now my loyalty was again going to be tested. I was ordered to take Philip out of the picture. So much for taking it easy and kicking back for a minute. I picked a couple of experienced members for the hit and set it up. I knew that my stay on the mainline depended on my staying out of the limelight, and I wanted to remain there as long as possible. Because I was being called on to set up all these hits, administration wasn't going to go for much of that. I had to be careful, that was my job.

I ran into Snake one afternoon and we kicked back and talked about the old days. We had known each other since we were kids. Snake and I reminisced about our earlier years and brought each other up to the present. It was a good talk, but Snake sensed I was uptight. He knew I took my job seriously and that's about all I was concerned with. He started telling me about his girlfriend, Lydia, from San Jose. He said she had a sister named Chris, who was really nice. He went on to tell me that she was available and looking for companionship. This took me by surprise. All I'd been thinking about was my responsibilities as an NF leader and what was going on inside. I told Snake that my job came first and I didn't really think there was room for anything else. He went on to explain that Lydia was coming to visit him all the way from San Jose and he didn't like her coming by herself, so Chris was coming with her.

The thought of being with a woman was very tempting, but I told Snake I didn't have time for any of that. There were just too many things on my mind. I didn't want to be distracted or let my guard down, even for a minute. That's just how it is when you're leading a bunch of guys and lives are on the line. So, he let it go.

On a Friday night, a few weeks later, all of the Lieutenants of the NF were warned about a BGF hit that was going down on one of their own. It was to take place Saturday morning. When a warning like this occurs, we all go on 'semi-alert' status, which means nobody walked anywhere alone. No less than two should be together at all times. If for any reason an enemy enters NF territory, we go on 'full-alert' status which means no less than six members together wherever anyone goes. Lieutenants have bodyguards around all the time, no matter what. It's called grouping, and when the prison guards see this grouping going on they're alerted to trouble, or at least to signs that something might be about to happen.

The hit was supposed to go down in F-wing, and we were housed right across the hall. With this in mind we were on full-alert status. Everybody was walking in groups, including the youngest member Baby-Goose. Goose was orphaned at birth, and when he got old enough he took refuge with NF. He's been with us ever since, and has a promising future as a leader.

After lunch on Saturday, we were headed down the hallway to go back to E-wing. Some commotion erupted in F-wing just before we reached the E-wing entrance. Something told me that we weren't going to make it back to the wing. That's when we saw black guy come staggering out of F-wing, holding his chest. He stopped and leaned against the wall right before he got to us, slid down and collapsed. He was dead.

That caused a mini Chinese fire drill. All of a sudden, my bodyguards swooped me up and we all ran like hell down the hall and into E-wing. Anybody in the way was pushed aside and everybody else scattered to make a hole for us to get through. We didn't want to get caught up in the web of bystanders who would be rounded up and held as witnesses or suspects. We finally made it to the furthest end of E-wing, caught our breath, and had a few chuckles over who all got their feet trampled in our retreat. It's gallows humor, a way of deflecting the scenes of violence we're exposed to, and a way of avoiding thinking about it in gruesome terms. It may seem callous, but it's a defense mechanism. Even in the face of death, life goes on.

Chapter 20
Chris

For the next couple of days we were on lockdown for the investigation of the BGF member's death. On the second day of the lockdown, Snake was bugging me about writing to Lydia's sister, Chris. We were locked up in the cells anyway, so I decided to send her a brief letter. At the last minute, I enclosed a visiting form, and within a week she had been approved. She was coming up the following Sunday with Lydia. I couldn't believe this was happening so soon. I hadn't even really been thinking too much about it. I hadn't been around any females for quite some time, for years. All I'd been concentrating on was my position in the NF, and staying alive and keeping the other guys alive. This was something completely out of the blue, and new.

When Sunday arrived and I was notified that I had a visitor, I wasn't ready to go. I was nervous about meeting Chris. Snake was already dressed and was waiting for Lydia. He came by to pick me up. When he saw that I wasn't ready he told me he'd meet me outside.

I started feeling a little anticipatory. There was a strange excitement surging within my chest. I hastily got dressed and pulled on a pressed shirt and pants. I had a nice pair of shined shoes I'd never worn. A quick glance into the mirror and I was on my way. Twenty minutes later, Snake and I checked into the visiting area and walked in. When I first laid eyes on Chris my heart skipped three beats and my throat felt like it was being squeezed by a python. Sitting there with Lydia was the most beautiful woman I'd ever seen in my life! She had jet black hair that came down to the middle of her back and looked like silk. Her light brown eyes were clear and amazing, and twinkled when she looked at me. The blouse she wore matched her eyes and the black slacks and open toe sandals complimented her looks.

As I walked toward her it felt like we were the only two people in the room. When we embraced her hair and perfume were so intoxicating that I forgot all about anything and everything else. When she hugged me a surge of adrenaline rushed through me. It was one of the most memorable moments of my life. There was a little girl with her that she introduced as Ilene. Ilene was six years old and took to me right away. Chris also mentioned she had an eight-year-old son. Eileen had her mother's eyes and smile. Chris was 26 years old, but didn't look a day older than her sister Lydia, who was two years younger.

Sodas and chips were bought and we went out to the patio area on the grass. I'll never forget that June summer's day. There was a light breeze and it blew Chris' hair all around. She was so beautiful and that scene only enhanced her appearance. Chris made me feel like a totally different person.

We talked and got to know one another. I wished to myself that the day would never end. But like all good things, soon we had to say goodbye. I wasn't sure what to do so I gave her a kiss on the cheek. I guess that wasn't what she had in mind, however, and she surprised me with a lip-to-lip, tongue-to-tongue kiss. Wow! That's what I call a sweet ending to a perfect day. Chris must have enjoyed herself as well, and she told me that she would be back to see me next weekend. She said she was going to bring her son, and as she gathered up her things I told her I would call to make sure she got home okay. As Snake and I watched the three of them go, I was thinking about how nice the visit had been and how I was feeling about Chris. As we turned and headed back to reality, I knew I had to get my mind back on my job. Tomorrow would be another day.

The following Sunday Chris brought little Ilene and her son, Victor, with her. Ilene ran right up to me and jumped up for a hug with a big smile on her face. Victor was a little shy at first, but after a few minutes he relaxed and started talking and asking questions about me. He was a smart kid, but he'd had very little contact with his father. The day was just as nice as the weekend before. Victor and Ilene played together while their mother and I watched and enjoyed each other's company. I started to think about my future and the possibility of becoming a family man. But I was still in prison, and I had other obligations… as a member and leader of the NF.

Snake informed me one afternoon that the brother of Lydia and Chris, nicknamed Lil' Smiley, was just sentenced, along with his crime partner, for an NF hit and murder. Snake and Lydia had been engaged for quite a while, and Snake knew how I felt about Chris. And he knew my intentions. He suggested that I talk with Smiley, and ask for his blessings and permission to marry Chris. At the time, it seemed like an appropriate suggestion, and I agreed with Snake. I'd wait and talk with Smiley. After Chris found out, though, she wasn't happy at all. That's because she's the big sister, and I'm not going to go all into that situation, not here.

Three weeks later Snake informed me that Chris's brother, Smiley, who was also an NF member was housed in C-wing on the first tier where all of the incoming inmates go for orientation. I went over to the wing to talk with him. He was a little guy in stature, and younger than me. This was the first time that we met, but he knew of me and who I was through his sister. Smiley and I hit it off right away and became instant friends. I explained how I met his sister through Snake and Lydia in the visiting room, and about my intentions to marry Chris. We made some small talk and he told me why he was in prison. I could tell that he was sizing me up as a brother-in-law. Then he told me I had good taste and that he knew Chris would be happy to marry me. He went on to say that he had no problem with me taking his sister's hand. He also mentioned that Chris wasn't too happy with the NF due to the fact of what had happened to him. I knew there were a few girls who felt the same way, but that meant little to me.

The following weekend when Chris came to visit I was the excited one who couldn't wait to propose. When I was called for visit my heartbeat doubled with anticipation. I knew what was coming. After a few moments of small talk, I dropped to one knee. With the whole visiting room watching I asked her to be my wife, to which she replied, "Yes,

I would love to be your wife!" We spent the rest of the day planning the wedding day. Her mother would come, and the kids. We'd have to sort through the paperwork needed and compile a guest list. It would be short. Lydia and Snake, Smiley and his girlfriend, Mary Lou.

Three weeks later on a beautiful sunny day we exchanged vows with each other, sealing a lifetime contract. I didn't believe in divorce. It was a nice wedding, with the wedding cake fit for a king and queen. That day will always be remembered. Later that week when Chris and I were alone, we got to talking about the NF. With Chris having firsthand knowledge of the NF from her brother, and knowing my background and rank, she was not surprised at all when I told her to never ever make me choose between her and the NF. I knew how she felt about the gang and I felt it was something she needed to understand. A lot of members were telling their girls the same thing, and a lot of them didn't like it.

I told her that if I had to choose between the two, I would choose the NF over her every time. Nothing more was ever said on the matter.

Chapter 21
The New Rule
1977

The businesses of the NF were expanding every day. And with expansion, came new rules designed to enhance our growth potential. A note was sent to all NF officers one Sunday morning to let everyone know to alert their families that the following Sunday there wouldn't be any visits with any members of the NF. No questions asked. Families were told that they shouldn't come and no reasons were given.

That following Sunday, all the NF officers gathered on the yard for a meeting. We were assembled in a circle with NF soldiers situated in an outer perimeter surrounding the officers. This was to keep out any other NF members as well as potential intruders. This was obviously an important meeting, how important I'd soon find out.

The effect that this meeting had on the organization was so impactful, so resolute, that it changed the entire fate of the NF in a single instant. It also changed the attitudes of many within the NF, some in a negative way. The new rule that was to take effect immediately was that from this point forward, there would be no more heroin used by any member of the NF, with an emphasis placed on the word 'NO'! To impress the membership of the seriousness of the rule, the edict proclaimed that anyone caught using heroin from now on was subject to a death sentence. This was automatic and without arbitration.

This new rule compared to the famous 'Shot Heard Round the World' that signaled the start of World War One. I asked DR why there was to be such a harsh penalty for using hard drugs when everybody was using them. He explained that it was for just that reason. Everybody, or most everybody in the organization was using heroin or hard drugs and it was bringing negative attention to the NF. These same people were using drugs and killing other people and committing crime behind drugs and drug use, and these actions weren't condoned by or conducive to the betterment of the organization.

The new rule caused some animosity in the ranks. Needless to say, the hit squad was working overtime to affect compliance with those who didn't take it to heart. The membership declined a little at first, but rebounded again as members finally saw the end result of ill ways, or put another way, saw the light of changing bad habits. With the change came increased profits and greater discipline. Within a few days six members asked to be locked up because of the new rule.

After the meeting, I returned to my regiment and informed them of the new rules, which elicited the same concerns which had been raised earlier. After being in the organization for several years, I was aware of most of the unforeseen problems and could pretty much nip them in the bud, but this was going to take it to a whole different level. I went on to explain that I didn't agree with this new rule either, but that I would follow it and sure as hell enforce it in the interest of the NF, even if that meant the punishment of death if someone was caught using heroin.

Two weeks later things took a bad turn for the Nuestra Familia. We had lost six members who had locked it up, losing face and going into protective custody. Then word leaked out that several members were under investigation for suspicion of using heroin, and it was known they were dirty. They knew what the penalty was and decided they didn't want to face the music.

Then somebody got really stupid and killed a kid named Blanco from Stockton in a drug deal gone bad. His death never should've happened. Because of it, shortly afterward the SSU and the FBI started arresting members and putting pressure on the organization, looking for Blanco's killer or killers. With this kind of pressure put on some of the high-ranking NF members, the unbelievable started to happen. Mousey broke down under threats, then Jesse James, then Art Vee. They all started talking and giving the feds information. Oh, they all received immunity and were put under the federal witness protection program, but they were also put on the NF most wanted list. The repercussions and fallout continued for the NF as the SSU and FBI started raiding our business dealings.

This caused the circumstances surrounding the organization to spiral even further downward. Because we were losing revenue at each shop, card room, hotel, and most all other money-making venues, they started closing down even before the feds busted them. This was a disaster and I was taking it personally. Some of my closest buddies, who I looked up to, were now outcasts and traders. I felt sick in my heart. The organization was falling apart.

A week later a General Council meeting was called and took place on the bleachers on the yard. This was not going to be a nice meeting. All the Lieutenants from all the regiments were in attendance and standing in a straight line, shoulder to shoulder, facing me on the bleacher's perimeter. Ten feet in all directions was secured by NF soldiers to keep the meeting private. I ran down the latest events that had taken place over the past couple of weeks, and about the Blanco kid getting killed, which triggered the fed investigation.

Then I lost my cool. I uncharacteristically lashed out at the members, expressing my disappointment of those who had broken the circle of trust in the Nuestra Familia. I ranted and raved until I started to go hoarse. I was so out of control that one of my Lieutenants approached and took me by the arm, pulling me aside and out of earshot of the other members. He gave me a stern warning, telling me to never talk to them like that. I was enraged at the time, but I also knew he was right. I told him that it wasn't personal. Did I feel better afterward? Not really.

Before the day was over I was summoned by Babo and DR. I pretty much knew what they wanted and I was right. I was reprimanded for losing my cool. I let them know that I was just voicing my opinion.

They told me to tone down my opinions, especially to those members who were still loyal to the NF. I finally simmered down and thought to myself that Babo and DR were right.

The next day, as if we didn't just go through enough, word came down that Larry was busted for killing a guy by hanging him in the county jail. He was on his way back to prison with the life sentence. I asked myself, "Is this all worth it?"

As the feds were dropping their hammer on the Nuestra Familia organization, members knew changes were imminent due to the new rules. The feds were coming at us with a new tool of their own called the Rico act, which has to do with organized crime. The NF had grown so large that the organization was split into two groups. The main group was called the 'Inner Circle', with the secondary group being called the 'Outer Ring'. These were people of an outside regiment who are all NF sympathizers. This new regiment was commanded by Bo, who had a Captain's rank. Bo made rank after all these years, and I knew he would be a good leader.

The Outer Ring would later be known as the Northerners. The reason for that Outer Ring was to keep the two groups separated, thus throwing off the feds from the Inner Circle. It was a sort of decoy to keep the pressure away from the higher ranks of the NF. Even though Bo was Captain, he answered to the General or the First Captain of the Inner Circle.

Anyone wanting to join the NF from that outer ring had to prove himself by committing an illegal act of the sort acceptable to the NF. That act could be selling drugs, stealing cars, pimping a prostitution service, or in some cases killing an enemy. Only then would a prospective member be considered by the General or the First Captain for approval.

(In 1982 the federal government indicted about 50 members of the NF under the Federal Rico Act.)

One of the assignments of the Lieutenant-in-charge of a regiment is to turn in a monthly report as to how his regiment is doing in regards to making money for the organization, as well as individual evaluations of members in the regiment. This is a 'must-do' task to keep the brass of the NF informed of the progress and logistics of each regiment. Lil' Richie from San Jose, in G-wing, came under scrutiny when he failed to do this task. He had been in the position of Lieutenant for just a few months and was doing what he could, but a lack of leadership skills was weighing on his shoulders. A motorcycle gang known as the Vagos was controlling all the gambling and drugs in G-wing. I was sent there because Lil' Richie had lost control of his regiment.

When I arrived, I told Lil' Richie that I was there to replace him. He had expected this to happen and didn't give me any resistance during the transition. He was demoted to Wing Commander, making him my right-hand man. He knew all that was going on in G-wing and until I was brought up to speed about everyone in the regiment, I needed him there.

Chapter 22
G-Wing 1977
The Beginning of the End

I set up a meeting with a guy named Rusty, who is the leader of the Vagos Motorcycle Club. We swapped a few war stories then got down to business. After listening to what he had to say regarding establishment of the gaming tables and the drug scene, I came up with another plan where I would start my own gaming tables. It would include supplying cigarettes, coffee, and music to make things more attractive to the clientele. It cost a little more in the beginning, but as business picked up, we started making money. It took us a month to get it established, including getting our soldiers in place for protection.

An alarm went off in F-wing, and Lil' Richie reported back that an NF member had been hit. My regiment immediately went on full alert status. I told Lil' Richie we would stay on full alert until I found out what happened. I sent him to find out what was up from DR. DR told Lil' Richie that 'BB' from San Francisco was hit and killed by two other NF members with orders from higher up. The whole prison went on lockdown for three days for the investigation. We did, however, get to go to the chow hall to eat. Then it was right back to our cells.

I kept Lil' Richie running to gather all the information that he could find. He returned hastily around lunchtime to report that he had talked with a guard who told him that the administration was going to pull all the NF leaders off the line and put them in the hole. After hearing this bad news, it struck a nerve. I started thinking about my new wife and family. The past few months had been nice being out of the hole, and I was not looking forward to going back there.

The three-day lockdown was extended to over a week, which was unusual. I received word that all the Lieutenants were being rounded up and taken to the hole, which was confirmed a day later when staff told me just to leave my stuff where it was. It would be picked up later. I was once again escorted to the hole.

One major problem with the administration implementing this plan was that without the leadership of the Lieutenants to keep order and discipline in each regiment, chaos within the ranks was inevitable and small problems would escalate into large ones. Unfortunately, Sacramento, which had ordered this plan, hadn't taken into consideration the bigger picture and didn't foresee the consequences of their actions. Their only mission was to eliminate the prison gangs from running the prisons, and to cut down on the murders and violence.

After I was taken to the hole on the second-tier, I reported to Black Bob, the First Lieutenant-in-charge. Being sent to the hole meant that I lost rank again, and was reduced to soldier status. Snake and Smiley, my brothers-in-law, we're just down the tier from me. A week later we all went to committee and were informed of Sacramento's plan to break up all the gangs by sending us to other prisons. What the administration seemed to have overlooked was that they were putting us in more danger, and thus creating a more explosive environment for everyone to exist in.

With all of us going to the hole the kites were flying back-and-forth. DR sent word that he'd chosen a guy named Chino from Baker to take my place in G-wing. I got back to DR and told him not "No", but "Hell no!" Putting Chino in charge in a leader's position was a bad idea because he was an idiot. I didn't get any reply so I thought to myself that DR would have to find out the hard way. And he did.

DR told Chino to continue running our gambling tables, the key word being 'our'. Chino must have had problems sharing when he was a kid, because he took the word 'our', and replaced it with 'my'. He thought everything was his and took it. The word greed comes to mind. Not knowing I had set up an agreement with the Vago's, Chino went to them and said that he was taking over the gambling tables. Rusty told him that this was not going to happen, but Chino was not listening.

Back on the mainline that following weekend there was a nice peaceful baseball game on the diamond. By the end of the game the score was NFs zero, Vagos four. Meaning that the Vagos had thumped on Chino and three other NF members with baseball bats during a fight… or should I say, contract understanding that I made with Rusty. It didn't make any difference with DR, as he, Crow, Rabbit, Dicky Bird, and I were transferred to Soledad prison to the hole on the hospital side. After being at DVI for seven years, and after only being married to Chris for two months, I was not feeling good about this move. Babo, Smiley, and a few others were transferred to Vacaville Prison to the hole to keep them isolated from the general population.

The bus ride from DVI to Soledad seemed to take longer than usual. Transportation had stricter rules now about being on the road. Those days of singing, dancing, talking, and listening to the radio were gone. Now you sat shackled and quiet during the whole trip. If we talked to one another, the transport guard would start yelling at us to shut up. If you were a trouble maker your property might get lost. Forever.

After arriving at Soledad and being held in the hole, we received more depressing news. Those of us involved in gangs were being put on the Director's caseload. That meant we could be kept in the hole indefinitely. As I listened to staff delivering this welcoming speech, my mind went to my family and how Chris was going to take the news. How would she feel about me now? I was feeling a deep hurt inside, like a big loss.

I sat down the first evening and wrote to Chris, telling her how sorry I was that this had to happen. I told her that I had nothing to do with what occurred to cause the move. But because the incident came from within the NF, and since I was a part of the NF, that's the way it had to be. Chris and the kids were very disappointed and hurt. I was worried that she might divorce me because of what I had told her about making choices between her and the gang. My heart was really with Chris.

Then one day something surprising happened. Black and white TVs were issued to each cell in the hole. The reasons for this were two-fold. First, the TVs are a distraction to those who are violence prone. Second, it's a sort of babysitter for those who are depressed or bored. In about ninety percent of cases they've shown to be a deterrent for negative ambitions.

Eventually the main reasoning behind all the moves that scattered us all to different institutions came to light. It had to do with the handling of the BB killing. It seems that BB wanted to branch out into his own free enterprise and start his own family. This action was considered a traitorous act by the NF, since BB was a member and was attempting to become a competitor with the family. The administration was looking at this murder within the NF ranks as the organization losing control and going too far. By instituting this action, it caused the beginning of the end of the Nuestra Familia.

Chris wrote me a couple weeks later and told me she was upset about the move also. She reassured me that she wasn't going to divorce me. That news lifted by spirits. We could have contact visits, but only in a special visiting room separated from the mainline population.

After being in the hole this time for three months with nothing to do, boredom came into play. This is expected in this type of setting. The mind is always working to keep you from going insane. When all these ticking minds are searching for something to do, two things can happen. One, it could be negative, like finding destructive projects to engage in, or two, it could be positive, taking our newly donated black and white TVs apart and tinkering with them.

There were a few guys that discovered quickly what wires not to touch, even with the TV unplugged. Being curious can sometimes be shocking. Eventually those of us who did have some electronic experience found a way to retune the TV receiver to pick up local radio stations and listen in. That provided a sense of accomplishment. We felt as though we'd gotten one over on the guards, even if it was a minor victory. Later, our little secret was discovered, and the TVs were sealed shut with the promise that if the seal was broken, we'd lose the TVs.

Dicky Bird had been chosen by DR to be the tier Lieutenant-in-charge. He was housed at the far end, I was in the middle, and DR was at the front. I considered Dicky Bird a good man and a friend, and had known him for about two years or so. One afternoon the normal din of noise was interrupted with a "man down!" call from the far end. That's a verbal alarm that someone needs serious medical attention. Staff arrived immediately and went to Dicky Bird's cell. They called for a gurney. When they rolled him out and he passed by my cell, I could see his skin was grayish. I had a bad feeling. He was taken to an outside hospital and word came the next day that he had died of a brain aneurysm. I guess it was just his time to go. He was well liked by everyone and would be missed as a friend and comrade.

We didn't have a group memorial service for him. Nobody wanted to let others see their feelings. But as individuals we said our private goodbyes and prayers for him and wished him a better life. He was free at last.

Life must go on, and when one member falls or leaves the organization, that person is replaced as soon as possible. DR appointed Crow as Dicky Bird's successor to keep the NF flowing as normally as possible. Of course, there was an investigation and an autopsy to make sure it wasn't poison or anything else that caused his death. While in the hole we went to the yard, which was mandatory. Everybody had to get some outside time, but it was just an excuse for staff to search our cells for knives and other contraband.

Chris came to visit me a few times and things seem to be going well. Because I was in the hole, I was not allowed family visits. This was causing a strain on our relationship and took a toll on both of us. I knew something had to turn around or my marriage was in danger.

Brown Eyes, Crow's wife, had been in town at the market and ran into a woman who struck up a conversation. The woman's name was Katlyn, and she was a sympathizer to the Nuestra Familia, and a producer of records. She mentioned that she was from Gilroy and was interested in making a record about the NF to help us out. On a visit with Crow one Saturday, Brown Eyes gave this information to Crow, who passed it on to DR. DR, after thinking about it, decided it was a good idea. To put it into motion he ordered Rabbit and me to go ahead and come up with the song, or the words to a song. I was hesitant at first because it was against the Constitution of the NF.

Another thing that I considered was that Babo, the General, had not given his okay to do this project. I wanted to ask Babo if this was okay with him, but not being in a position of rank to do so, I would have been stepping on DR's toes. I didn't want to get in the middle of a situation between DR and Babo.

For one thing, I wasn't in charge at the time, so it wasn't my responsibility. Two, I'm no fool. Maybe DR had already received approval from Babo and hadn't shared this information with me.

Two months later a member named Chongo, who was musically inclined, along with Rabbit and myself, came up with the words to the song of the Nuestra Familia. The three of us were real pleased with how this song came out and were anxious to hear it on a record. An agreement between Katlyn and the NF was reached, and the song was sent to Katlyn on the streets for it to be recorded. Two weeks later the record hit the streets and was a hit among the Mexican population. Profits from sales started to fill the coffers. Then someone came up with the idea of putting out T-shirts with the NF logo on them to be sold on the streets. Even more profits were made.

Again, I was thinking all of this was against the Constitution because of all the publicity that was putting the NF name on Front Street. The constitution says "there is no NF". That's why I didn't like what was going on. I knew that Babo wouldn't approve of it, especially considering how notorious the name Nuestra Familia had become.

During a visit from Chris she brought something to my attention about the other wives and girlfriends. They were talking in whispers to their husbands and boyfriends in the organization the past few weeks. Then she pointed out that the wives and girlfriends were suddenly all driving brand new cars to visits. There was something out of place in this picture. Members were spending money beyond their means, which meant more than likely it was coming out of the NF Bank. It didn't take a fool to reason that out.

During a visit, Brown Eyes told Crow that the NF members on the street were told to disregard any orders from DR inside the prison. Crow passed this information on to DR, and I could see from his eyes something was wrong. It sent up a red flag. I became suspicious about this news and started asking questions as to who initiated this order and why. Something was not right and I was determined to find out what it was.

After another two weeks of this activity of secrets floating around, a kite was sent to me from DR. A piece of hacksaw blade was tucked inside. I had orders to make a hit, and the blade was for me to cut through the coarse material of the security screen to get a piece of metal to make a knife.

At the time, I wasn't given the name of the hit target. What I found out years later was that DR felt that I was sending information to Babo about what DR was doing.

A couple of days after I was given the order to make the knife, the Institution Security Unit (ISU) came to my cell and escorted me down to the committee room. Upon entering out saw welcoming party of assorted staff which included the FBI, SSU, ISU, the Warden, and someone from the District Attorney's Office. I was asked to have a seat at the end of the table. The DA broke away and approached me, leaned over, and in a low tone asked me what my rank was with the Nuestra Familia. The following dialogue ensued between myself and the DA.

DA: You deny being in, or a part of, the Nuestra Familia?
Joey: Yes
DA: Have you ever killed anyone?
Joey: No
DA: So you've never heard of the NF?
Joey: Nope, can't say that I have.
DA: I'm sorry to hear that. I was going to make you a deal if you gave me some names and information. But since you never heard of the NF, I'm going to charge you with eight counts of murder, committed over the past several years.
Joey: You can't do that! You're just fishing around! You've got no proof of anything against me. I've done nothing wrong, so I guess I'll see you in court.

With that said I got up from my chair and left the committee room without saying another word. I was escorted back to my cell by staff. DR was next to be called out and escorted, presumably to the same committee room for the interrogation and offered the deals that were made to me. DR had always been a very loyal and dedicated leader in the organization. I'd never had any doubts about him, ever.

I was starting to have an uncomfortable feeling inside of me, though. Too many things were going wrong within the organization, and I couldn't quite put my finger on it. And with orders to make that hit, from DR, it didn't make any sense. I wasn't happy about the hit, but being a soldier, I follow the orders of my Captain. DR knew I would never fail him and he knew my loyalty to the NF. It took me two days to cut out the piece of metal for a knife. What happened next raised the red flag up another notch in my mind.

I let DR know I finally had the piece of metal he asked me to acquire. Then, he gave me the order to sharpen it. This just never happens. A single person is never given the job of procuring the raw material, sharpening it and stashing it, all in one place. Unheard of! This wasn't right but I didn't argue with DR. I followed orders like I was supposed to. It took all night to sharpen the knife.

I finally received word that the target of the hit was to be a black guy, my neighbor, who I'd never had any problems with. He was targeted for something he did against the NF at another institution. After I finished with the knife I hid it behind the sink. The hit was to be made that coming weekend.

Then DR did something that was uncharacteristic of a leader. He asked me where I'd stashed the knife. That red flag warning in the back of my mind just elevated another notch higher. The bad feeling was getting worse. Again, I didn't challenge him on the matter. I followed orders and reluctantly told him where I had hidden it. Something was telling me to get rid of that knife, or at least move it. But my loyalty and trust in DR stopped me. Later I would regret ignoring my inner voice. I told DR I was going to the yard for a while. On the way out I stopped by his cell to see if he was coming. He said he wasn't feeling well and stayed in. I told him I'd see him later and headed out.

Outside we had an informal meeting and I told everyone that DR stayed in because he wasn't feeling well. Everyone accepted this except me. The nagging feeling and suspicion wouldn't shake. My red flag warnings were about to come to pass.

I'd been outside for about an hour when I was called to the gate by staff. They told me that the facility Lieutenant wanted to see me in the committee room. A chill ran through me when I heard this. I was escorted there and when I entered the Lieutenant didn't waste any time telling me I was being charged with "possession of a knife". I denied it and said I didn't know anything about but the Lieutenant wasn't buying it. He informed me that this would be a D.A. referral and asked if I had anything to say. I told him no.

I was escorted back to my cell and when I passed DR's house noticed it was empty. I asked the guard escorting me if he knew where he was. He told me that DR had locked it up, meaning he went into protective custody. All my suspicions were confirmed in that instant. DR had turned traitor. I called Chris with the bad news, and the worse news that our contact visits had been pulled, at least until after the DA referral hearing. She took it okay, but it was obvious from her voice that she was disappointed.

The next morning was routine. After a breakfast of pancakes, hot cereal, a banana, and coffee, it was clean up and get ready for the yard. An hour later the bars opened and we left our caves to be escorted outside for some sunshine and fresh air. We assembled and had an informal meeting. Crow had the higher rank. He said he hadn't heard anything from Babo yet, and we were kept in the dark about any investigation. When DR locked it up, it caused psychological panic within the ranks. With all of DR's years and knowledge of the organization, he was a huge liability.

Just when we thought the red flags were at their highest level, we found out three weeks later that there was still one more notch to go when Babo showed up in the hole with the rest of us. He'd been transferred from another institution for unknown reasons. Nobody ever asked why the General had been transferred and no reason was given. It just happened.

When an organization is under scrutiny and suddenly the General appears, everybody takes a deep breath and hearts skip a beat. Paranoia sets in and it gets mighty quiet in the regiment. A kite came down the line saying that our regiment was under investigation due to money missing from the NF Bank. This meant everybody, including me, was being looked at as persons of interest. I took offense to this, personally, because of my sincere loyalty and devotion to the family.

There was a blanket restriction on all incoming and outgoing mail, especially me, because I have numerous contacts and brothers-in-law in the organization. If I ever needed anything to be done or checked on, I had the resources to do so.

A week after Babo's arrival he was cleared and approved to go to the yard and mingle among us. Just having him there rattled those of us who were feeling guilty. He passed the word that he would be talking to each one of us individually to see if we knew anything. He explained that some money belonging to the organization had come up missing and since he was in the neighborhood, he would start investigating with our regiment. He was going to talk to Crow first, then the rest of us one at a time.

When it was my turn to talk with Babo I told him about the new cars the girls were driving to visits to see their husbands and boyfriends, and about the record being made and sold for profit. He said he did approve the record deal, but he didn't know about the T-shirts, which meant that even more money was missing. Babo was not a happy camper and got even more upset when I told him about the hit I was ordered to make, as well as the DA referral for possession of a weapon, which just happened to be found after I told DR where it was. Babo said he had no knowledge of this hit to take place.

Word came down later that the reason why my once good friend DR set me up to have me removed from the yard was that I had knowledge of his activities regarding the missing money. This confirmed my suspicion as to why DR had locked it up. Babo confided in me that he knew about the eight counts of murder against me because the DA had told him about it before coming here. I was still angry about being investigated by the family, and wanted to know why, considering how loyal I was to the NF. I wanted to keep Chris out of it completely, which I managed to do. At the time things weren't looking good for me.

Babo went on to tell me that the missing money had been intended to go to the regiment to be used for NF projects as needed. Instead it had been funneled into DR's personal fund to be used for his attorney's fees for the embezzlement case he was facing. That's why DR locked it up, I thought to myself. He wasn't the only one. Those nice new flashy cars the girls were driving around came to mind, and a week later Crow, then Legs Diamond, did the same and locked it up into protective custody.

One by one, the higher ranks of this NF regiment started falling out of the organization: Jesse James, Mousey, Crow, Legs Diamond, and DR. With this news word came back from the DA that they, and others, were giving away valuable and sensitive information about the organization. This was all behind the investigation of the killing of that kid, Blanco, that had just gotten out of CYA. He'd been suspected of using drugs. This later became known as the Stockton Incident.

This was not good. The infrastructure of the Nuestra Familia was slowly breaking down and the future of the family was looking questionable. Over the next few months I became closer to Babo, and he acknowledged the confirmation of my loyalty to the NF and to him, which made our relationship stronger. He had appointed Rabbit as Lieutenant to replace Crow when he turned traitor. Rabbit was doing a good job under the circumstances. It looked like my leadership days were over, and believe me, I didn't have a problem with that.

Rabbit's wife and my wife were coming to see us on visits together and they soon became good friends. Rabbit felt comfortable enough with me that he felt he could trust me. One day when he was giving me a haircut, he confided that he had enough information to bring impeachment charges against Babo, and the other Captains, over issues of money and their misuse of power. Rabbit said he thought he'd bring this to my attention due to my loyalty to the organization. I explained to him that I go by the Constitution and didn't care about all that other bullshit. And if anyone went outside the Constitution I would, without question, address the issues and take the appropriate action, even if it meant eliminating that person. Not long after that conversation, Rabbit was put on a list to be transferred to DVI, Tracy.

A few days later, at six in the morning, a guard came by my cell and announced that Babo and I were going to court in Stockton for arraignment on the eight counts of murder alleged by the D.A. We were flown from Salinas to Stockton for court. We lifted off in a twin-engine Aztec Piper that seated six. The one hour flight was uneventful and smooth. The sights from the plane were colorful, especially the reflection off the water from the lakes and rivers four-thousand feet below.

As we flew, Babo struck up a conversation and asked my opinion of Rabbit. I thought back on what Rabbit had told me about the impeachment of Babo and the other Captains. The thought was disturbing and I felt uncomfortable sharing this information with him because it might be construed as tampering with an investigation, if there ever was one. I told him I was against his choice. All I could do was convince him to select another more qualified candidate for the position, without letting him know my reasons. He seemed to be comfortable with my opinions and took them into consideration.

When we landed in Stockton and taxied in, I saw a black van with two police cars waiting along with several police officers. They would be our escort to the courthouse. As we neared the courthouse we saw there was tight security surrounding the building and for a block in every direction there were police cars and cops. Every fifty feet there was a heavily armed officer on alert for any type of breach. Due to our position at the very top of the NF, we needed this extra security to prevent other gangs from trying to take us out.

We turned off the main road and proceeded down an underground driveway that led underneath the courthouse. Several Sheriff's Deputies and a Marshal awaited our arrival. From the van, we were escorted to an elevator that would take us to a holding cell on the second floor.

Soon thereafter we were taken onto a courtroom for arraignment. We entered to find it filled with numerous media, all taking our pictures and taking notes for news stories. We were seated in a boxed-in secure area while awaiting the attorneys appointed to us. They seemed anxious to defend us. We just sat there and waited our turn.

One young attorney, who introduced himself as Jim Hill, came over and told me he had just graduated law school. I was on trial for my life and wasn't too interested in having an inexperienced attorney defending me. I asked to talk with another one. I noticed an attorney who looked like he was older and more experienced. He apologized and informed me that was just appointed as a judge, but he did have someone else in mind, his wife, with twenty-one years working as a lawyer. I told him that sounded fine. I'd be glad to have her represent me. Introductions were made and I was set for the battle of my life.

My new attorney, Pat, hired the rookie lawyer, Jim Hill, as an investigator on our team. He brought us news that the D.A. had seventeen known NF informants testifying against us, which was not good. They said the trial would take a while. It ended up lasting five years.

At the end of the first week we were flown back to Salinas, and then driven to Soledad prison. Babo and I were enjoying all the air time. With all the mileage, we could have acquired significant frequent flyer miles. Eventually the trial and transportation costs were really mounting up. Somebody had to be keeping tabs. The D.A.'s investigator suggested that to keep costs down, Babo and I could be housed at a prison closer to the courthouse. Vacaville Prison was chosen because it was only an hour away. This was good news for me. Chris was much closer this way and didn't have to travel far for visits! I called to tell her the good news. She was just as excited as I was. This was long overdue. I couldn't wait to see her again.

When Babo and I got to Vacaville we received another surprise. We found out that Larry and my brother-in-law, Snake, were also there. They filled us in on the place and we all brought each other up to date on what was happening. We were glad to be together and we were all housed in the same tank. The food was better, with three hot meals a day. We could also have contact visits.

We were housed in the High Security Unit, or 'High Power', as it's known. There were six tanks on the tier, with five individual cells in each tank for a total of thirty convicts per tier. At the far end was housed one of the most infamous convicts ever, Charles Manson, who master-minded the killing of the movie star Sharon Tate and her houseguests in L.A. We didn't earn the same notoriety as Manson, so we were housed near the front of the tier.

During the daytime we were allowed some outside time on a small yard, and I do mean small. It was more like a patio, but it was better than nothing at all.

About seven o'clock one-night Babo called a meeting of the three of us. He told us the he'd received word from Soledad. It seemed that

Rabbit had succeeded in impeaching Babo, Larry, and Snake from the organization. But Rabbit had some heat on himself for some of his actions, and the Impeachment Committee turned around and was scrutinizing Rabbit as well. I wasn't sure what I was going to do if the committee found them guilty of anything.

At the time, I had enough on my plate to worry about with the upcoming trial, which carried the death penalty. I was also thinking about Chris and how she was going to take all of this. I knew she was worried. The impeachment of the leaders was the least of my problems, or so I thought. The impeachment process would take years for the investigation to be completed, which I was unaware of at the time.

One day, Chris came to visit and she told me that she had a kite from her brother Smiley, and it was 'For My Eyes Only'! I opened the letter and read it. Smiley's brief message contained disturbing information. Babo was found guilty of interfering with an investigation, and Rabbit was not found guilty of anything. It didn't take a fool to see what was happening.

The real shock was yet to come. The next paragraph said that I, Joey, was informed that orders were given to me that I had sixty days to execute Babo, Larry, or Snake for the above finding by the Impeachment Committee. I was furious about these orders and knew I would probably get in trouble for sending a message back to the committee telling them that I wasn't going for this B.S.

I also told them I would get back to the regiment and talk with the investigation committee. I felt that this so-called investigation was biased against the three as they were unable to defend themselves due to their absence. The action Rabbit took against Babo and the others confirmed my opinion of Rabbit (to myself and Babo). Rabbit didn't make any friends by showing his true colors.

Chapter 23
My Emotional Tool
1980

I was beginning to feel the pressure and experiencing extreme anxiety from all that was going on in my life. My emotions were torn between my wife, the trial, the impeachments, and basically being taken out of the day-to-day simple existence of prison life. I asked Babo if he knew who these eight guys were that we were being accused of murdering. He didn't answer me at the time. I wanted to know: who, why, and what for, because I had no clue who they were or even what regiment they were in. The only thing I knew for sure was the fact that the D.A. had the testimonies of seventeen former NF snitches against us. Other corroborating evidence put us in the spotlight and had us on the hot seat. I asked Babo how we were going to fight this case with such a gloomy outlook?

He explained that because of the way the Constitution was written, there was no Nuestra Familia. And with no NF, we couldn't win because we could not defend ourselves. So basically, we just sat there with nothing to say for ourselves and accepted whatever the outcome was going to be. This trial was just another bump in the road, and life would go on.

Meanwhile, Snake was taken back to the California Institute for Men (CMC) at Chino. He later dropped out, with others who would not testify against us. The regiment at CIM had disbanded, and soon other regiments would follow in their footsteps as leaders began dropping out. Nuestra Familia, as it was once known, was failing. It was failing because of the greed of one person that led to the killing of a youngster. This was not a sanctioned hit, and it brought public heat on the Family. This had turned into a media circus and we were the clowns in the center ring.

The first of the trial came and went. My relationship with Chris was strained, at best. This was hard for her and showed when she came to visit me. I thought back to one day. My last day with her.

The visit seemed to be going well, but I sensed something was wrong. As we were saying goodbye, she broke down and started crying. She wouldn't tell me what was wrong and I started to feel bad inside, real bad. I felt it in my heart. I truly loved Chris and it was real. I loved her with all my heart, but my immature and selfish dedication to the NF was in our way. I tried to call her later on, but my calls were unanswered.

A month after her last visit, another hammer fell on me. I was served divorce papers. This was just another hit in a long line, and bad timing for me. I understood, though. If Chris had only known what was going on with me, what I was going through. The pain of losing her was overwhelming. It was obvious she didn't know the circumstances because we never talked about it. I didn't want to worry or burden her with details of the NF. Now as I think back, if I had shared my prison life with her, would she still be with me? I'll never know.

The trial was taking a long time and costing a lot of money. The county was starting to cut corners to save dollars. One of those ways was to cut down on transportation and man-hours on extra guards to take us back and forth from Vacaville. Soon Babo, Larry, and myself were transferred to a newly refurbished section of the county jail, saving travel costs and other expenses. So much for our scenic trips outside of the cage.

The newly built section of the jail was made specifically for the three of us. It was located away from all the other inmates and had three individual cells with access by specially assigned staff only. This also eliminated all contact visits, not that I was expecting any. My only visits now were from my attorneys.

As the trial progressed and evidence was presented against us, I was having doubts in my own mind as to why these guys were even killed. I didn't know any of them, yet I was being accused of being a conspirator in their demise and presented as a leader who gave the order to have them killed. The truth was that the guys testifying against us were the real culprits in these crimes, the same seventeen pointing their fingers at us. As each day went on it became more and more clear that we were fighting a losing battle. I was looking for some loopholes, anything, any chance at a dismissal or mistrial.

During a courtroom break, Babo and Larry asked me what I was going to do about the Impeachment Committee hearing. There wasn't much I could do now. The fact was that I had more knowledge concerning the issues than the Impeachment Committee, and I might be able to turn their verdicts around; however, my priority was to complete my trial. Then I could get back to DVI to present the evidence I had in favor of Babo, Larry, and the others. I told them I'd do everything humanly possible to help them out and not to worry about it now.

Basically, their lives were in my hands from the same Nuestra Familia that they had dedicated their lives to. Even with the future looking ever so gloomy during this period in my life, I was continuing to prove my dedication to the organization. This was because of what I believed in, and I had to stay strong.

Babo was looking troubled, but wouldn't share what was bothering him. His pride was standing in the way. He too was standing strong. The same went for Larry. We didn't break or give up any information for any reason. I knew this was making the D.A. angry and more determined on doing what he set out to do, to make and present a solid case against us and make an example of the three of us. With all the publicity, he was earning political capital and making the most of it. He was milking it for all it was worth, and the media and public were eating it up in steaming mouthfuls.

The trial continued for a few years, bringing up this and that about drugs for sale, gambling and card clubs, prostitution houses, and on and on. This brings us back to the beginning of the story, where I was sitting in the courtroom holding cell, waiting for the jury to come back with the verdict after a five-year-long trial. It was 1982 and I was waiting to know if it would mean the rest of my life in prison, or would I be another condemned convict waiting for that fateful day to come? Guilty or not guilty is the question.

But wait! There's more to the story. Remember, the last General is still standing.

Chapter 24
The Christmas Party
1983

Here it was December already. I heard staff talking to each other about Christmas shopping for their families. My Christmas spirit was in the bah-humbug stage. The jury was out for fifteen days before returning a verdict. After the first week of deliberations, my attorneys were very much in the spirit. They asked the judge for permission to bring in outside food for a Christmas party at the courthouse, which he granted. My spirits were lifted when the various foods arrived. There were burritos, chips, soda, beans, potato salad, and all kinds of pies. There were lemon pies, banana pies, coconut cream, and pumpkin pies. That kind of food was never seen in prison and tantalized the palates of the three of us. Even the clerk of the court had it in her heart to bring a homemade lemon meringue pie to share with us.

Not everyone thought badly of us. A camera was allowed in and Christmas pictures were taken of everyone. My attorney even brought me some new clothes to wear. For the first time in a very long while I sincerely felt a warmth in me. There were a couple of court bailiffs there for security, but that Christmas party was a welcome distraction from what had been going on for the past five years.

Babo, Larry, and myself ate to our hearts' content and got pig-stuffing full. It was one Christmas party I will never forget. Our attorneys picked up the tab for everyone. As the party ended and we said our thank you's for such a memorable afternoon, we talked and joked all the way back to our cells. We had bulging bellies and smiling faces.

That night we drifted off content, forgetting about all else.

Three days later the jury came back with the verdicts. We were brought in and seated with our lawyers. I looked over at the jury, trying to read their faces. I was anxious to know my fate. We all stood as the bailiff announced the entrance of the Honorable Presiding Judge. Everyone was seated. The courtroom grew hushed with dead silence as the jury foreman handed the verdict form to the bailiff, who handed it to the judge.

The three of us stood with our attorneys for the pronouncement. Camera shutters clicked and flashes exploded with bright light. Here were the pictures to go along with tomorrow's headlines. Then the verdicts were read. The counts were split evenly among us. We each received four counts of murder. After the verdicts of guilty were read, the three of us agreed and told our attorneys to waive our appeals and get on with the sentencing phase.

The judge pounded his gavel several times to quell the noise and obliged us with his edict after the commotion had died down. The following sentences was pronounced for each of us, separately. I received four, seven-years-to-life sentences, one for each count, to run concurrently with the life sentence I was already serving. I took a deep breath, turned, and thanked my attorneys for saving my life. For an instant my mind lapsed back to the memory of the day we went to the hole for this very crime.

And now after five exhausting years the trial was finally over. I felt like the weight of the world had been lifted from my shoulders. I hadn't received the death penalty, and that was good news. The bad was that I added four more life sentences to the one I was already serving. People who I had gone to battle for, guys that had been part of the organization I dedicated my life to had turned traitor and testified against the three of us. They did it to look out for themselves. In a time of need you find out who your true friends are. At thirty-four years of age, those life sentences seemed like an eternity to me. But then, in my mind, my heart and dedication was still with the Nuestra Familia. It was all I knew and lived for since my late teens. I took a deep breath, shook it off, and held my head high.

After being sentenced we were escorted back to our cells. When the evening meal came around I didn't have much of an appetite. None of us did. It was quiet that night. Nobody was in the mood for chatter. GAWD! The rest of my life in prison lay ahead of me. I was feeling so lonely at that moment. I was thinking of Chris and wanted somebody to talk to. I wanted to share the news with her. I missed her enormously. Then I had another thought. I didn't get the 'life without the possibility of parole' sentence, so at least there was the possibility of release some day.

Chapter 25
After the Trial

With the trial behind me I was looking forward to going back to prison again. A few days later though, and we were still in the county jail wondering why we hadn't left yet. I overheard a couple of deputies talking. They said the CDC didn't want us back. Now that was a first, but early one morning the County Sheriff loaded the three of us up and drove us to Vacaville prison. They dropped us off like a bag of puppies and made a hasty exit. Once there, it was obvious that the administration didn't want us around other inmates. They feared we might be a bad influence on them. Because of who we were, the prison wasn't set up with the kind of security needed to house us. We were temporarily housed in Ad-Seg until they could figure it out. Within a week of our arrival, our transfer orders came in. Because of the notoriety of our case and our status in the organization, they didn't want us housed together. Babo got his traveling orders to DVI Tracy, Larry went to Folsom, and I ended up going to San Quentin. Within a few weeks, we each went our own way.

When I got to San Quentin I was treated like a leper. They didn't want me in their prison, either, so I was housed on death row with the condemned convicts. Whenever a new arrival comes to new prison, he is automatically put on orientation status for fourteen days until he is seen by committee and housed appropriately. I was seen by a guy I knew from Soledad North a while back. He had been promoted to Program Administrator, and oversaw the facility. He went over my colorful, no, my very colorful central file at committee, and it was determined that I would be held in high security for the next eighteen months.

I had no contact with anyone on death row or with anyone in the Family. This was the first time I was by myself without any NF. When I got to the small yard for exercise, there was a BGF member there and he was telling me about East Block. There was a gang there called the Northerners. I wasn't familiar with them. I talked to staff about a move to East Block.

For the next uneventful and long eighteen months I was on death row. When I was finally approved for the move to East Block, they put me on the second tier, ten cells from the front. It's a fifty-cell tier and most of the inmates were kids, or maybe I was just getting old. I met a youngster named Toro from Modesto. He was bright and carried himself with strength. Toro reminded me of myself when I was his age.

After a couple of weeks, I took him under my wing. I told him I was NF, and he told me he was in a group called the Northerners. He then told me that because I was older and more experienced, and due to my former rank in the NF, I was in charge. Everyone on the tier was in acceptance of this suggestion. Toro mentioned that there was another older guy they all thought was a little off in the gray matter area. His name was Tree and they said he was an NF sympathizer, and that he seemed dangerous. The others stayed away from him. I told Toro that I wanted to meet this guy.

After being on orientation for two weeks I was finally released by the committee to go to the yard. I was given a grand tour by Toro and the rundown on Who's Who. I needed to get word to people on the streets and let them know where I was, and that I was back in circulation again. Babo was still the General even though he was at DVI Tracy. He would straighten all this out as our communication came back on line through the grapevine. My current duty was to organize the second tier and start a new regiment from the ground up, as the Constitution outlines. That's what it was designed to do, to maintain the integrity of the organization.

As mentioned earlier, the Northerners were born, or established, as the outer ring to act as an undercover shield to protect the inner ring of the NF from investigation from the authorities. Toro gave me little by little a breakdown of their group, and how this offshoot branch of the NF had come to be at San Quentin.

I went to the yard after breakfast one morning and met Tree. We introduced each other and like a couple of old dogs, sized each other up-and-down. We took a walk around the yard and he told me that he was forty years old and ex-military Special Forces He was about 6-foot-three and kept himself in good physical condition. He had received a fifteen-to-life sentence for a shootout with the Oakland Police Department. Nobody was hurt or killed; he said he was just high on drugs and spaced from flashbacks of the war. And yes, he was as dangerous as a rattlesnake.

Nobody liked him and they kept their distance. After we talked and I got a better understanding of him, I took a liking to Tree. I guess it was because he was a soldier and we both shared similar interests. He also accepted me as his friend. Tree was later released after serving his time, and a couple of years later died happily while having sex. Meanwhile, I appointed Toro to be my right-hand man. He had already proven his worth, and I saw in him the same enthusiasm and dedication that I had at his age.

One afternoon while out on the yard, I asked both Toro and Tree to meet with me for a few minutes. Both guys had what it took. I had gotten to know them and had seen their dedication to me. So, on this sunny, clear and smoke-free day, I recruited both Toro and Tree into the Nuestra Familia. I was able to train and mold the two of them into good soldiers. My new and expanding regiment was off to a good start.

One Friday evening at around seven o'clock, six months into schooling and building this new regiment, my spirits took a lift when Babo, the General of the Family, showed up in East Block. It had been over two years since I had last seen him and I was glad to see him now. He was glad to see me, too. We brought each other up-to-date and he told me he had gotten into a fight at DVI, so he was transferred to Quentin. He didn't go in to details and I didn't ask, other than the report he provided upon his arrival. The report is always expected from an arriving high-ranking member to the ranking member in charge. And because this was the General who was arriving, he too, expected a full logistics report of the immediate regiment which consists of the following information:

1) The status on each individual in the regiment.
2) Why they are here, details of what happened, how long a sentence they received, and whether anyone was hurt or killed.
3) Individual likes and dislikes, future plans, and full evaluations on each member.
4) How many weapons (knives) are available and who is holding them.
5) Allies - BGF and any others; Enemies - EME and AB, and others in the immediate area.
6) The schedules and times of yard, program, chow, etc.

This report was due five days before Babo was to report to the facility committee. Talk about thoroughness. This is a definite sign of a well-run organization, one that will be around for years to come.

Soon afterward other members started showing up at San Quentin: Casper and Cricket from Salinas, old man Joker, a guy by the name of Wayne who was the first white guy ever to be allowed in the NF. And other members, about 10 or 15, who didn't agree with the decision of the impeachment committee to impeach Babo. I knew that all hell was going to hit in time, but I had to wait and see.

An impromptu election was held and I was elected to be Captain of the re-investigation of the first impeachment. This was mainly because I had knowledge of more complete information that the first committee was completely unaware of. The new information would change the outcome of the verdicts. Everybody was warned that absolutely under no circumstance was anyone to stab or start any act of violence during this re-investigation. Anyone who went against that order would be considered to have engaged in an act of treason and held accountable for interfering with an investigation, and would be dealt with accordingly.

With myself as the elected Captain of the new Impeachment Hearing, word was sent throughout the state to other regiments in other prisons of this fact. It didn't take long for word to get back. Three weeks later Robert from Stockton came down from Old Folsom and informed me that I had overstepped my boundaries in re-opening an already dead issue. He told me that the regiment at Old Folsom did not accept that I was reinitiating a new hearing and that they accepted the current decision of the committee. Also, the Folsom regiment would not go along with any decisions made by a new impeachment committee.

When I received this information, it was clear that they had already made up their minds and were not interested hearing the truth, not even the facts of why this impeachment was brought about in the first place by Rabbit. So much for trying to do the right thing and bringing things into perspective. In the back of my mind I knew I had ruffled some feathers, but I didn't know how badly at the time.

At this point in time the tension among Nuestra Familia members was starting to build. I had been assigned to the lead porter position of East Block and oversaw laundry, inmate feeding, and other related tasks. Basically, I was given unfettered movement throughout the block and unlimited access to any of the five tiers in the building. I had hired Toro as my right-hand man because he was loyal and capable. Between the two of us, we knew who had the knives, where they were stashed, who had drugs and when they were coming in, by whom and from what visitors.

I knew of every kite in East Block and what was in it, and more importantly, who came into or out of East Block for any reason. With this new information from the P.A. about all the NF members being moved to San Quentin, a great big red flag went up the pole. I gave everybody a heads-up concerning the moves and ordered everyone to start making weapons and stashing them to the side, just in case. I knew that reopening the impeachment investigation could bring heat, and it could get downright bloody.

I sent word out to the regiments, trying to explain Rabbit's motivation for initiating the impeachments, and tried to explain why others hadn't accepted the reasons. It only fell on deaf ears. It seems that Rabbit was from Gilroy and was surrounded by some of his homeboys and others from Gilroy who supported Rabbit's decision regarding the impeachment proceedings. Later they would be known as the Gilroy Boys.

For the next six months arguing went back and forth with a few troublemakers behind the scenes. It was obvious that Rabbit had set his sights on the General's position for himself when Babo was found guilty. It was all part of his agenda. But, blinded by ambition to be the next General, he didn't see the bigger picture that was unfolding right in front of him. The Nuestra Familia had disbanded all the ranks and replaced them with the Meza (table), which was to include only six members to act as leadership of the organization. In time, they would learn that something like that doesn't work.

In East Block a covert meeting took place on the second tier to plan and execute a hit on a couple of troublemakers. It was an effort to bring them back into line and quit stirring up mischief by beating the war drums. To keep from drawing attention, we went to the far end of the first tier and went up the stairs to the second tier, and to the last cell. That's where the meeting was to take place, right across from the cell where Tree lived.

Tree, one of our own, was playing both sides of the fence. This was discovered when he 'accidentally' let it slip to the opposing party of our plans to hit the malcontents. The opposition then armed themselves for battle based on Tree's information. Damn his loose lips. If Tree only knew. The fuse he lit would ignite an explosion that would bring down the General.

The hit was set up after Tree returned from visit, which included him bringing in drugs from his visitor. It was cold and wet that day from a storm coming in off the Bay. It was typical weather for this part of the state and everything seemed normal out on the yard. The morning came and went without any problems, but the afternoon brought the hurricane of events that are described in the next few paragraphs.

The tension was as thick as San Francisco fog on the yard as the afternoon rolled in. You could smell it in the air. If you've ever been in that kind of situation, you know what I'm talking about. You're aware of it in a sort of sixth sense manner, but there is no one thing you can put a finger on. The feeling is inescapable. By 3 o'clock yard recall, it was like electricity and I wasn't the only one feeling it. Everybody returned to their cells in prep for the evening meal. After a brief body pat-down, we were allowed into the building and headed to our appropriate tiers.

Toro and I were the last ones in so that we could start our jobs as porters on the first tier. Casper was going to the cell on the second tier, and bent over to pick up his shower bag when it kicked off. Two guys came up behind Casper and started stabbing him. He turned and started fighting back, getting in some good work on his assailants. Toro heard the commotion and looked up in time to see Casper get stuck. He got my attention and I looked up. He told me Casper just got hit.

We both grabbed the rails and started a vertical climb toward the second tier to help Casper. Meanwhile, also on the second tier, Babo had just left Casper's cell and turned back to say something when he saw what was happening. His adrenaline went into hyper-flow and he launched at Casper's attackers with the voracity of a wild bear protecting the family. Babo's concentration was so focused that he didn't feel the wounds he received as he pulled one attacker off Casper and threw him down the tier walkway. Then he noticed the knife still stuck in his back. He pulled it out and tossed it over the rail toward Toro and myself as another attacker was heading our way.

The melee continued as the guards sounded the alarm, alerting other guards who arrived with shotguns loaded with birdshot. One of the responding staff saw Toro and me in mid-ascent and fired a round of birdshot. It struck a steel beam to the right and ricocheted onto both of us. It caused us to fall about ten feet to the floor below. That birdshot hurt like hell. I don't care what anyone says.

We were both OK from the fall and scrambled up in time to see the knife that Babo had tossed. It dropped next to Toro. The attacker headed for us was a little late to the party. I yelled for Toro to grab the knife, and he got it in time to turn the knife on the assailant. The expression on the enemy's face went from anger to surprise and fear.

He did an about-face and ran toward the three individual security cages at the end of the hall. He locked himself in one of them; in other words, he peed on himself. We were rushing him when another guard saw our intent and yelled for us to hit the ground. We complied. All around us knives were being tossed like confetti in all directions to get rid of them. Not all were successful. Other shots were fired to bring the free-for-all to an end.

When the smoke had cleared and the dust settled, Toro and I were escorted back to our cells in cuffs. As I walked by Casper's cell I could see blood all over the place. He had been stabbed in his left shoulder and the artery had been hit in his leg. That's where most of the blood came from. He was placed on a gurney and carried to the infirmary where he was stitched up. He survived.

Babo proved to be one stubborn, tough dude. He had been stabbed in the chest and in the back. Luckily, they'd missed all the vital organs. When the gurney arrived to take him to medical, he looked at it and then at the guards and said, "This is nothing. I won't go out this way." He got up and walked himself, under escort, to the infirmary where he was patched up and lived to fight another day.

That night after cell-feeding I had plenty of time to think. The whole East Block was unusually quiet. Even the crickets seemed to sense things weren't right. They were silent as well. I sat there on my bunk just staring at the wall. I was feeling despair, the feeling of a leader who lost his way to lead. There was now a big split in the organization that was going to take a lot more than a Band-Aid to fix. I knew that I couldn't do anything.

I could see the rift that was dividing the members and others, and it was only getting worse. I was thinking to myself, "Why am I fighting?" I'm too damn old for this stuff. Nobody wanted to hear the truth, or at least the ones who should be listening didn't want to hear it. Is it worth it all? I found myself torn. I was caught up in a power struggle that would undoubtedly lead to more violence and bloodshed. While I still felt a strong dedication to the cause personally, because it's what I believed in, I was conflicted. Such were my thoughts as I drifted off to a fitful sleep.

The next day brought more trouble for Toro when he got stupid and stabbed another inmate through the bars of the cell for threatening him the day before. This got him a D.A. referral and moved to the first tier on total lockdown status. I lost a good right-hand man that day.

I received a letter from Robert. He apologized about the hit Babo, and said that Casper was the target. He went on to say that the original impeachments cannot be undone, and must be acknowledged and accepted by us to prevent future retaliation. He said that nobody wanted it to go this far. When I finished reading Robert's letter I was still angry and upset. I didn't immediately respond back. I wanted to wait until Casper and Babo returned from the infirmary and had healed from their wounds.

The PA called me into his office and informed me that the administration was considering separating the youngsters from the old-timers if we couldn't get along. The administration didn't have a clue that this fight wasn't about a generation gap, but rather an in-house dispute. It made no difference to them what the reasons were, though. They just wanted the violence to stop.

Five days later Casper and Babo were released from the infirmary only to be moved to separate yards. They were not coming back. All of us were being sent to committee for re-housing to other yards to break us up. The administration thought this would help to quell the violence. I flat out told them I was not moving. I had been here in this prison a long time and had helped the administration keep things in order with the NF. This was my yard and they owed me big time. They finally yielded to my request and let me stay. Cricket, another old-timer, also got a free pass to stay, probably to keep me company.

As time went on, old man Joker cashed in his mind when he took some new high-tech drug known as a 'hotshot'. He went into convulsions and then into la-la-land. He never came back. Joker was killed by his cellie at Corcoran State Prison. Wayne completed his term and was paroled to his new life and was never seen again. Two-timing Tree was moved to the yard Babo and Casper were on. I'll bet the move made Tree uncomfortable.

Most of the moves had been completed and the yard had a lot of new faces. Younger faces, meaning a new generation. Another two weeks came and went. I had started to get dirty looks from some of the youngsters on the yard. I'd been doing a lot of thinking about what Robert had written me in his letter. It was haunting. I'd always been dedicated to the NF and been loyal to Babo. This impeachment was a festering sore on my saddle. I knew I was right in trying to bring the truth to light. I believed that with it, it would overturn the verdicts of Babo and Casper and expose Rabbit for what he was. To what end was I willing to pursue this further? How many more brothers were going to be maimed or killed due to my insistence to prove myself right? Yeah, I thought the same thing.

After all these years plotting, planning, and fighting, it was time to throw in the towel. I was just tired of the fighting and bickering, and looking over my shoulder everywhere I went. I was tired of all the responsibilities involved. And worst of all, I was tired of losing good friends. My time as a leader of the Nuestra Familia had come to an end.

I sat down one evening after chow and wrote a letter to Babo letting him know I had made my decision to retire from the NF. I explained to him and reminded him of all the past good years we'd had, but it was time to bail out. I was tired and it was starting to show. Babo and Cricket both tried to talk me out of quitting and keep the investigation going, but both finally realized I was adamant about my decision.

Babo reminded me of the going away party, meaning the ass-kicking I would have to endure for leaving any gang I was in. I told him that after all my 17 years of dedication, if they felt that this was the way it had to be, then bring it on. I just didn't care anymore one way or the other. My mind was made. Gawd! It's a bitch to say goodbye.

Cricket finally caved in and understood where I was at, and accepted my decision. He told me he would have my back, but I wasn't looking for him to do that. The Family was business, not personal, and everyone knew that. I went to the yard to inform everyone I was through and was resigning from NF. Not a good move on my part.

One thing about leaders and gangs, when one leaves for any reason there are at least ten others waiting to take his place. Hector from Salinas just happened to be one of those guys bucking for status and position. He approached me on the yard one morning after my retirement speech and told me I couldn't come back to the yard anymore. I looked this wannabe gangster in the eyes and without a flinch told him when you have walked in my shoes for as long as if I have, then and only then, will I allow you to tell me I can't come out to this or any other yard. With that said I turned around and walked in another direction, leaving him speechless and red-faced. I don't think he liked being put in this place, especially by an old-timer. I wasn't trying to disrespect him or anyone, but I just wasn't going to let someone talk to me like that.

One morning on the yard I noticed a guy named Lil' Joker doing something out of his normal routine, which was usually sitting around shooting the bull with others in his little group. Joker was running in circles on the track. This guy never runs anywhere, let alone jog. It was so out of character I just knew he had a knife wrapped up in his hand, and was waiting for the right moment as he built up his courage to do what he had to do. I could have took it to him, but for what? He has his orders and now it was up to him to follow them.

Cricket came out to the yard and joined me as we waited for the supervisor in the laundry truck to arrive. A few minutes later, a guard shouted to us that the laundry had arrived and we were needed by our supervisor to come unload it. We were walking across the yard when Cricket was called over to where a group of four others were standing and talking. I kept heading for the gate. This was a ploy to get Cricket away from me and he didn't pick up on it until it was too late. I wasn't as alert as I should have been. That is until it was too late.

I was focused on the task of the work ahead of and didn't even duck when I felt a slight brush from behind, then the warm trickle of blood coming from above my left eyebrow. I brought my hand to my face and confirmed it was blood. I looked around and saw Lil' Joker damn near flying on air to get away from me. My adrenaline kicked in and as I turned to give chase with the intent to do some severe damage, the guard noticed the blood on my face and yelled at me to stop where I was. I did.

Another guard saw what happened and came up to me. I had a black sweatshirt on and he noticed that it was saturated around the collar. Upon closer examination, it was discovered I had a cut across my throat. The weird part about it is that I didn't feel the cut when it happened. The assailant was good at what he did. I just didn't know how good he was. The cut across my throat was deep, almost too deep. I was in shock, induced by pride in part, but foremost by bleeding on the inside.

I grabbed a clean towel from laundry and put it around my neck to stem the blood flow. I had reached the rotunda of the yard where the guard called for a gurney for me. I told him I didn't need it, when it arrived they talked me into it. I said I wasn't lying down, so I was carried to the infirmary sitting up. I guess I had forgotten I was in prison and had not stayed focused on what was going on around me.

While en route to the infirmary I was swallowing a lot of blood and my lungs were filling up at same time. I was hurt worse than I thought I was. I was starting to have trouble breathing. When I arrived, the medical staff saw my distress and turned me on my side. Now, as they turned me, panic overwhelmed me as I started to vomit nothing but blood from my stomach and lungs. I started to see stars floating around in my eyes as my skin got damp and clammy. Then the lights went out and I lost consciousness.

When I woke up a few hours later, the first face I saw was a Catholic priest leaning over me. Something told me I should've gone to confession more, and now it was too late. The priest told me I had indeed died and he had given me last rites. I looked up at him and said, "No, not yet." But then I thought, God's not finished with me yet because I woke up. My mother and aunt came to see me and be with me at the hospital. They had been called because the doctors thought I wouldn't make it. But I reassured my mom that I was okay and that I would see her again at the prison visiting room.

I spent five days at the outside hospital before being released back to the prison. Then I spent another five days in the prison infirmary ward. While resting and recuperating I started to think again, 'why?' Here I was, stuck, stitched, and now convalescing. All this after giving seventeen years of my life dedicated to the NF. All I wanted to do was retire, quit, and go away. It's not like I was asking for a gold watch or anything special. If I had a clue that this was the way a senior dedicated leader was going to be treated, I probably would have considered a different retirement plan. But, I knew what I was getting into seventeen years ago, when I joined the NF. There was nobody to blame but myself. That's life in prison.

After the fifth day in the infirmary, I was returned to East Block where I kicked back and relaxed. Within two days I was back before the Institution Committee and informed that due to my age, thirty-seven, I was being moved to the integrated yard where Babo and Casper were. I agreed with the decision of the committee and was moved by the end of the day. Cricket was already over there. He'd been moved for his own protection and because of his age.

I know what you're thinking. We got moved to a geriatric ward or yard. Let me tell you this, back on that yard maybe we did sit around, but it was at a meeting where we declared an all-out war on anyone from the yard from which we'd come. Furthermore, we would take any one of them out on site. Of course, anybody from outside the prison group who saw this probably thought a bunch of old geezers had made a suicide pact. We are talking about a bunch of very seasoned NF members who were more venomous than a pit of vipers. Those youngsters would get first hand schooling if given the opportunity.

Then one beautiful, sunny summer day a couple of months later, karma occurred, or should I say opportunity happened. Somehow, the administration had inadvertently transferred two young gangbangers to the integrated yard. Oops! The new arrivals were already on the yard, which is the size of half a football field. My tier was the last to be released. The two gangbangers were at the restroom area, which has a four-foot brick wall surrounding it for a little privacy. There's no roof and it's open so the guards can see the area. As one youngster stood point, the other was on the commode in the process of removing a knife that he had secluded in his derrière. That's got to be uncomfortable.

In the meantime, a guy named Sundown from Oakland had recognized the two from the other yard and ran over to tell me about the newcomers. As I came out I saw the whole yard of convicts lined up on the opposite side, the length of the yard and the width at one end, staring intently at the commode area.

When the two youngsters finally realized what was happening they got very anxious and wide-eyed. It looked like a pack of wolves circling their prey. The guards noticed what was happening and let it unfold before them while they watched with interest.

Then at the drop of a hat, seven to ten convicts broke out of the line, with Sundown in the lead. They headed right at the two guys. The youngsters stood their ground with defiance, putting the bravest face on they could muster, but knowing it was the last day they'd ever see.

A guard fired his mini-fourteen rifle and hit Sundown in the leg. I saw him go down and ran over to pull him back as more warning shots were being fired. Everybody hit the ground as if it were rehearsed. One of the gangbangers tossed the knife that he'd carried around so uncomfortably for so long. Staff ended up finding it, however. After the dust had settled there were no casualties or other injuries that day, except for two very soiled boxer shorts. That was one day I know of when two lucky guys truly appreciated the guards. As long as they live, I bet they'll never underestimate old-timers again.

After that incident things calmed down a lot, and we were once again getting back to normal. A new prison, California Correctional Institution at Tehachapi, opened. It was specially designed for gang members only. It was a new design with only two tiers per building, some with built in satellite kitchens between two buildings. It was all enclosed.

Everybody knew they were leaving San Quentin. Babo was sent to Tehachapi, and Tree had gone to Folsom. The gangbangers from the other yard were moved to CCI also. Cricket paroled, but came back with a twenty-five-to-life sentence. That left scatter-brained old man Joker and myself, the only ones left. Because everyone was being transferred to other institutions, and with new people coming in to replace them, for the next few years I lost contact with everyone. I was lonely. I also lost contact with my wife, family, and the old NF crowd. I had no ambition to continue down this path or to be involved with the organization.

Then it was my turn to leave. I was bounced around from one institution to another and eventually ended up at the California Medical Facility at Vacaville for the next three years. Finally, I was released back to the mainline. That was a nice change. Everything was going fine. I was working at R&R and doing okay. Then in 1990 I screwed up again and found myself in familiar surroundings. I was back in the hole over for over-familiarity with female staff. That caused me to be sent to Folsom where I ran into Babo and Tree. I was happy to see Babo again, and he was too. I recalled what Tree had done years before and wasn't so enthused to see him. Babo picked up on it and later asked me about that. I told him I'd tell him when the three of us were all together.

A meeting was arranged with just the three of us and I pulled no punches. I got right to the point about how reliable and varied sources had confirmed that it was Tree who let slip to the opposing party about the confidential meeting we had about setting up a hit on them. This in turn was the cause for Casper and Babo getting stabbed in East Block.

Tree was outed and he knew it. He stuttered for excuses and failed, but didn't deny it, either. From that day forward, I've not spoken to Tree. Babo, on the other hand, harbored no ill feelings toward Tree, even after knowing the facts of what had set off the violence that day that ended up getting him stabbed. Babo told me it's just something out of the past, to let it go. It was basically just the three of us now, the last of the original senior NF leaders, and we should stick together. I went along with Babo's reasoning, but this did not mean I had to talk to him or be his friend. I just put up with him.

After two years as Folsom, I noticed that Babo was getting thinner and losing weight. I mentioned this to him and he said he was just getting old. He wasn't feeling ill or anything, but did put in a request to see the doctor for an annual checkup. The doctor ordered tests and when the results came back he was called to medical. I ran into him on the yard when I brought him extra food from my kitchen job. I asked him what the doctor said. He told me he was going in for some exploratory testing, a biopsy on his esophagus. The next week he was taken to the hospital for the biopsy, and two days later he returned.

When I got off work that evening I brought him some food to try fatten him up. He thanked me and put on a cheery face, but after twenty years of knowing someone you can see right through the façade. No matter how much food I brought him, he continued to lose weight. I was getting more and more concerned.

We were on the yard one evening and when they called the in-out line, he told me not to go in, so we walked the track. I could sense he wanted to talk so I just waited. He dropped the bomb and told me he was going to die. I tried to laugh that one off. We were always kidding one another, and I thought he was joking around. Not this time, though.

Babo was like a brother to me and always had been since the day I met him. He told me about the exploratory biopsy and how when the doctor opened him up, they discovered he had cancer in his throat, probably from all those years of smoking. His condition was made worse when they opened him up. It made the cancer spread faster.

They told him there was nothing they could do, and gave him three to six months to live.

Even after he told me I didn't want to believe it. He's my friend, my brother, and I kept telling myself he wasn't going to die. But the look in his eyes confirmed it was true. I felt great sadness overcome me as the gravity of the situations sank in. He gave me his wife's phone number, just in case.

Babo also considered me part of his family. He told me to find Larry and transfer to where he was so that I wouldn't be alone. He wanted me to be with someone I knew when he died.

Babo made trips back and forth to the hospital for treatments. His spirit was high, but his weight kept dropping and he was getting thinner. In the last few weeks he could hardly talk because of the pain. He tried to keep a smile on his face but his darkened eyes and loss of weight told a different story.

On December 7, 1941, the Japanese bombed Pearl Harbor, pulling the us into World War II. Admirals and Generals were called into action to defend the United States. This date was also just as important for another kind of General.

I was on the yard that morning and after a while, Tree came up and told me that Babo had gone to the hospital. An hour later I was called to the program office and the P.A., a guy I knew from DVI Tracy, told me that Babo had died. I was shocked to hear those words even though I knew to expect them. He said he was sorry, and I thanked him for telling me privately. When I left the office, I was numb and lost for words.

I knew people were all around me on the yard, but at the same time I was totally unaware of any noise or sounds from anyone. I felt a welling tightness stir in my head and chest. I headed for the bleachers which I noticed were empty at the time, and sat down to think about what had just happened. My mind went into rewind through all the yards and good times Babo and I shared from the time he took me under his wing. He trained me, and through his guidance taught me to be a leader. My anguish and compassion for my brother flowed from my eyes as I grieved heavily into my hands.

After a few moments, I looked up out onto the yard through tear-filled eyes. The yard seemed to go completely empty before me. Then, one by one, old dead soldiers started to appear off in the distance, coming closer. These same soldiers I fought side by side with for what we believed in and trained for all these past years. They were soldiers that I had loved and respected for so long, that were no longer with me. They all looked at me with smiles on their faces as if to say they won the battle.

And then Babo appeared before me as he had looked in his younger years. He stood proudly with that look of the General that he was. And then I remembered something Babo once told me, a quote from another famous General.

"OLD SOLDIERS NEVER DIE, THEY JUST FADE AWAY."

To Order Copies of

THE LAST GENERAL STANDING

send $14.99 + $5.00 shipping & handling
or
3 books of 20 forever stamps to:

LWL Enterprises, Inc.
4475 Trinity Mills Road
P.O. Box 702862
Dallas, TX 75370

(Please allow 4-6 week for delivery)

Made in the USA
Coppell, TX
15 July 2023